To Julia, Joy, and Harrison
and
Amanda, Bibi, and Callie

Our households have been happily "cluttered"
with love and chaos because of the six of you.
As you grow up to be on your own, we hope we've
given you ways to find extra time for yourselves
in this fascinating—and hectic—world we live in.

organize
your life

free yourself from clutter
& find more personal time

RONNI EISENBERG
WITH KATE KELLY

John Wiley & Sons, Inc.

Published by John Wiley & Sons, Inc., Hoboken, New Jersey
Published simultaneously in Canada

Wiley Bicentennial Logo: Richard J. Pacifico

Design and composition by Navta Associates, Inc.

For general information about our other products and services, please contact our Customer Care Department within the United States at (800) 762-2974, outside the United States at (317) 572-3993 or fax (317) 572-4002.

Wiley also publishes its books in a variety of electronic formats. Some content that appears in print may not be available in electronic books. For more information about Wiley products, visit our web site at www.wiley.com.

Library of Congress Cataloging-in-Publication Data:

Eisenberg, Ronni.
   Organize your life : free yourself from clutter and find more personal time / Ronni Eisenberg with Kate Kelly.
        p. cm.
   Includes index.
   ISBN 978-0-471-78457-9 (pbk.)
   1. Time management. 2. Orderliness. I. Kelly, Kate. II. Title.
   HD69.T54E57 2007
   650.1'1—dc22

Printed in the United States of America

10 9 8 7 6 5 4 3 2 1

contents

part three
the "get it done!" system: how to do everything faster (and better) and fit the things you want into your life

part four
make time at the office: from the paper burden to everything electronic

part five
make time: you and your family

introduction

Time—don't we all wish we had more of it!

I don't need to tell you that twenty-four hours per day is all we get. The trick is to make the most of our time. You really do have time for what you need and want to do. You just need to start setting priorities.

Most of my clients find that they are so overwhelmed by all the daily "junk work" of life—that is, the errands, the phone calls, the picking up, the putting away—that they lose track of what they really want to do. Whether you'd like more quality time to spend with your family, time to set aside for yourself so that you can go back for an advanced degree, or just enough time so that you can read a book (uninterrupted) now and then, I'm here to promise you that these are achievable goals.

When I began writing this book, I didn't want to write just another time management book. I wanted to write a book that answered the question that I am increasingly hearing from my clients: "How can I find more time just for me?"

This book offers you innumerable ways to find more time for yourself. I've consulted with so many clients over the years that nothing surprises me anymore—from offices you can barely enter because of all the paper to houses that look like they ought to be boarded up and condemned, I've seen it all. I've also visited clients who live in a tidy environment but spend so much time keeping things well organized that they never get to have any fun. That's no good either. With these clients, I work on maintaining organization systems with a minimum of time so that they can still lounge around and watch television or go out to the movies or see an opera.

I've written this book so that you can benefit from all the experience I've gained in working with clients over the years. All that is required of you is to simply start out by making some small changes—you'll soon see the benefits.

As you can tell from the book's subtitle, *clutter* is the number one impediment to our having more free time. Thirty-five years ago, little girls might have twelve to fifteen dolls; boys might have a train set and some model cars. Siblings would share blocks and games. If you have children today, you know that most kids are drowning in hundreds of possessions—and so are we! This wealth of riches is actually stealing our time, and one of the purposes of this book is to help you regain control of your time by conquering your clutter.

If you are ready to dive in for a real makeover, start with part one, where you will learn all the basics necessary to begin regaining more of your time.

If you're looking for some quick fixes, go right to parts two through five, where I offer specific methods for doing things better. Select the area of your life you find most vexing, and dive in to the corresponding chapter and start making the adjustments I suggest. Later on, you can read through part one, as the basic skills explained there can make a big difference in your life. I've had many clients desperately say to me, "just help me straighten out my _____ [desk, files, calendar system, basement, kitchen, etc.]" so I know how people feel about getting started. Sometimes you just have one area that is driving you crazier than anything else.

Throughout the book you'll find special sidebars: "Quick Starts," "Sanity Savers," and "Time Boosters." The information in these sidebars will help you out when you're feeling desperate. My favorites, however, are the sidebars that offer "Mini-Vacations." We all need those now and then!

The wonderful thing about a book with helpful advice is that you can keep it around for a refresher course. So organize what you can now, and when you begin to feel as if your life is slipping out of control again, come back to the book. You'll find that as you begin to adopt more and more small changes, each time you begin anew, organizing your life becomes easier.

part

one

make time

planning and priorities

1

eight steps to regaining control of your life

We all know there are only so many hours in the day, but one of the reasons why we feel we don't have enough time for ourselves is that we *let* time run away without us.

You already know that you're feeling time-pressured and stressed, so rather than spending several pages explaining why you are feeling so badly (and wasting your time in the process), I'm going to jump in with solutions to help you begin finding time for yourself right away.

The secret to finding the time you want and need is to take control. Here's how.

step one: *track your time*

If you are like most of my clients, you would like to be able to snap your fingers and instantly gain more time. Unfortunately, we all have responsibilities, so immediate change may be what we want, but it's not always possible to achieve. You *will* find the time you crave, but first there is some work to do.

Tracking your time to discover what is happening to it is a very easy and beneficial exercise. Within a week, you will be ready to start making some changes. By simply going through this process you might become so aware of time-wasters that you could be ready to make some changes by later today!

You've probably heard of keeping a food journal when you're trying to adjust your diet. The same philosophy works with identifying how you are spending your time. It is difficult to determine how you can better manage your life if you don't take a look at what is happening in it.

Create a time chart for one full week to document how you are spending each twenty-four-hour period. Keep track of what you do on a half-hour basis. Note everything from showering and eating to e-mail and errands. You need to track your weekends as well. I've rarely had a client who hasn't remarked to me: "I just don't know where my weekends go." Well, now you'll find out.

Some people like to highlight their time charts with colors to better visualize how their time is distributed among various pursuits. You might select four colors to highlight work time, home-related tasks such as errands and chores, family time, and finally time spent doing something just for you.

Although creating a time chart may sound like it will take a lot of effort, it's really not that difficult once you set your mind to it. By the end of the week you'll begin to understand where your time goes.

step two: identify goals

During the week that you're keeping track of your time, you also have another assignment, which is to reevaluate your priorities. Although we all have certain priorities that we are committed to and that take up a lot of our time, such as work or family obligations, you bought this book because you aren't finding time for something that is important to you, so start listing what you would do "if only you had time."

This list's contents could range from getting a massage to going back to school to earning additional professional accreditation. Write down anything and everything you think of. Once you have finished, you'll begin to see what is missing in your life. For example, if your list is about twenty items long and five are items like "Play tennis more often," "Get to yoga class more regularly," or "Take time for Sunday walks," then you obviously need to find more time for exercise.

Although this "I wish I had time for . . ." list will provide you with several short-term goals, you should also think ahead—first, five to eight years ahead to take into account what your dreams are, and then two years ahead to see about changes you would like to make on the way to achieving those life goals.

five- to eight-year goals

This should be your "dream" page for your long-term goals. Write down what you would like to be doing five to eight years from now— for example, working in a different field, raising children, or retiring. Take several days to consider what you want your future to hold, and then settle on the one or two long-range plans on which you'd like to focus.

Be specific as you note your goals. If your goal is to learn a new language, do you want to speak like a native or to learn enough phrases to get by? The more specific you are, the easier it will be to act on your goals.

two-year goals

Record on the next sheet of paper what you would like to be doing in two years. Perhaps you would like to switch careers or to have more time for a specific hobby such as photography. If your long-range goal requires advanced education, such as going to business school or getting a Ph.D., then you should write down what you need to be doing during the next one to two years to accomplish this long-range goal.

Research may be required before you can move ahead with a goal. If you don't know the steps necessary to get an advanced degree or to become a life coach, for example, you will need to investigate the requirements before knowing what steps you need to take to prepare for this goal.

step three: evaluate your time and your goals in preparation for some changes

In step three you are going to combine the work you have done in steps one and two.

First, we're going to take a look at your time chart. Awareness is the first step toward change. If you have highlighted your activities by color as previously described, you'll be able to quickly assess certain factors. For most people, job and family are going to take up the bulk of their time. Although those are usually "givens" in our everyday lives, you can still take a closer look at both of those categories. If your workday is extended because of overtime or a long commute, are there remedies? For example, you might prefer to bring work home or ask if you can telecommute one day per week rather than stay late at the office, or you might have a long-term goal of moving closer to your job, which would save you commuting time. Family activities are generally time well spent, but even there you might consider whether responsibilities are appropriately shared. For example, your spouse might be able to pick up the children from day care at least one night per week to free you up to take a course or go to the gym.

Take a look at your time chart and consider these questions: What percentage of your time is being spent in areas that are not on your priority list? Where are you spending too much time? How can you be more efficient or cut back in the areas that are less important? All of us also find that chores, errands, home paperwork, and home miscellany take up a lot of our time, so this book is filled with suggestions for reducing time spent on the busywork of life. But there may be other changes as well. Perhaps you've been cleaning your house yourself but a recent promotion means that it would be possible to hire someone to clean twice a month. Think about changes like this one that would make your life easier.

step four: make your goals manageable

Set priorities so that you can focus on the most important tasks first. Otherwise, you might invest your energy in insignificant matters instead of what is most productive. To establish these priorities, look at your two-year and your five- to eight-year goals as well as your "I wish I had more time for . . ." list that holds your short-term goals.

Plan how you will make your goals manageable by breaking each one into smaller steps. If one of your short-term goals is creating a more nutritious way to feed your family without spending a lot of time on it, you might want to take a class in healthy cooking or visit a nutritionist for a consultation on how to make some simple changes in your meal plans. A longer-term goal such as moving to a new community would involve researching the job market, contacting real estate agents, investigating schools (if you have children), and so on.

Set realistic deadlines for various steps on the way to reaching your goals. There is something about a "finish by" date that makes a task very real. (A goal without a deadline can become nothing more than an unfulfilled New Year's resolution.) If you want to join a health club and haven't investigated any yet, write down a deadline in your notebook for having called or visited three or four.

(If you're fairly certain you still don't have the extra time you need, keep reading. I have a lot of solutions—both in this chapter and in the rest of the book.)

Plan to reward yourself for meeting deadlines. Mini-rewards such as a new paperback book or meeting a friend at your favorite coffee bar can be things to promise yourself for achieving several small steps and can provide a nice boost for work well done.

Review your goals weekly, selecting a reasonable number of tasks to undertake during the upcoming week. Realize that you can do anything you want, but you can't do everything. Be selective.

Stay on track. Sometimes circumstances prevent us from following our own priorities. For example, your child is sick, so you have to reduce your workweek, or the boss has required extensive overtime, meaning that you've missed some of your night classes that are part of another goal. When you need to tend to other matters, just do what you can to get back to your priorities as soon as possible.

step five: simplify with systems

The two primary ingredients for better time management are keeping an objective eye on what is wasting your time (step one) and remaining mindful of your goals and ideal lifestyle (step two), and then combining these two in steps three and four.

If you'd like a sports analogy, these first four steps are your offensive plays. Because there are so many things pulling at us for our time, the rest of the book will focus on "defense!" And trust me, you need to stay on top of your defensive maneuvers, otherwise you'll be flat on the field because you've been laid low by clutter, whining children, other people's priorities, and all those "should do" things to which we sometimes fall prey without considering our own responsibilities and preferences.

Step five is your first defensive maneuver, and the message here is "simplify with systems." Systems are perfect for all the tasks that must be done but aren't original, creative, or gratifying—such as grocery shopping, packing school lunches, weekend errands, and so on.

A system can be as simple as a grocery list (see chapter 9) or as regular as the fact that you are always on time with your bills because you pay them on the last weekend of the month (see chapter 11). (Actually, almost all the chapters in this book involve systems.)

Systems allow you to do things automatically so you don't have to spend time figuring out how to complete certain routine tasks. Once you have a system, you'll find you perform the chore almost reflexively. You wouldn't dream of forgetting to pick up milk because you always do it on Tuesdays and Fridays, and your bed is always made because you do it as soon as you get up. Systems require time to create and discipline to maintain, but they make life much easier in the long run.

Whenever you are stuck on how to accomplish something, think about creating a system. Although the process may go a little slowly the first time you do a particular task, you'll find that your pace will speed up as your system becomes familiar.

These are the things you should do when going through a new task.

- *Notice the current flow of the process.* This way you can maintain what works and refine what slows you down.

- *Create a beginning and designate an end.* From cleaning a room to doing a work project, structuring the job will help you to stay on task. For example, weeding out your files could be a huge job, to the point that it could consume all your free time. Instead of setting yourself up for failure because you've become so overwhelmed, you might opt to clean one drawer each month. That way the job gets done, but there is a beginning and an end to the project within a reasonable time frame.

- *Think sequentially.* If you intend to clean the garage, start on one side and work clockwise. Don't hop around. An orderly attack will help you to keep track of your progress, and it will be rewarding to

sanity  saver

TAKE BACK THE WEEKEND

Americans are working longer hours and taking fewer vacations. Evenings and weekends are often spent catching up on work, cleaning the house, or taking care of errands. Instead, you need to take back the weekend and make it be the break in the week that it is supposed to be.

For many, the ideal weekend is spent with family or friends. Others like to do something completely different from their weekday routine, whether it's community work, trying a new recipe, or taking a class.

If you have to do some errands, catch up a bit on some work, or squeeze in time for a dental cleaning, just make sure that you limit the time on these must-do activities. If weekends are to provide a respite from the week, you need to plan for a break and build in the fun you want to have.

In addition, schedule actual down time. While the idea of scheduling time to relax seems counterintuitive, it's actually necessary, or most of us will let that peaceful time slip away. So whether you want to nap, putter in your garden, or put on your MP3 player and listen to music, plan out some time for relaxing and enjoy it.

look to the left of where you park and see what great progress you've made.

- *Make the process become organic to the task.* When you get up in the morning, you can adopt the habit of automatically making your bed and hanging up your pajamas so that these things don't need to be done later. The moment you step into the office, you can do three or four things that need to be taken care of immediately upon arrival—such as checking your e-mail, reviewing your to-do list, and listening to any voice-mail messages that came in overnight. If a work crisis comes up shortly after your arrival, you've at least taken care of the basics.

- *Designate tasks.* If other people are involved in what is to be accomplished, make sure that responsibilities are outlined and that there is a method for the handoff of the task—whether it's getting the kids ready to be taken to school or preparing the monthly report for the staff at the office.

- *Include checkpoints.* Depending on the task, set deadlines as to when other people should check in with you, or set a time when you want to reevaluate how this particular system is working for you.

- *Write it down.* Any task that is slightly complicated—or one that you don't do frequently—can be written down in steps. The information sheet you create can be kept as a handy reminder.

Here are some quick basic systems you can implement right away that will not only make it easier to get things done but will make you feel as if you are giving your brain a vacation.

- *Keep ongoing lists for groceries, drugstore items, and weekend errands.* (Grocery lists are covered in more detail in chapter 9.) You'd be amazed how much better you feel when you aren't trying to remember things all the time—and by writing them down, you will find that you get them done. This will eliminate those times when you arrive home only to discover that you forgot to purchase something you need for the next day.

- *Keep a personal notebook with a running list of everything else.* (This master notebook system will be fully explained in chapter 3.) From vacation destinations you'd like to investigate to recommendations for books to read to a gift idea you are considering for your mother, keeping an all-in-one-place running list of your life makes everything easier. Although some people prefer an electronic list in their handheld PDA or computer, I think a lot can be said for a one-inch three-ring binder. You can create categories that represent the different parts of your life; also, a notebook is very adaptable.

- *Use tickler files.* Tickler files are your "action" files—that is, your future to-do list with backup copy, such as tickets you need for an upcoming trip or a memo for an office meeting on Monday. This system provides a logical way to locate needed items and reminds you of things you must do or calls you must make on a specific date in the future. To create tickler files:

Select thirteen file folders and labels. For a color-coded system, select a specific color for this group of files.

Label a folder for each of the twelve months. Label the remaining folder THIS WEEK. (Clients in office settings often like a tickler file for each day, so in addition to the monthly set, they take thirty-one additional folders and mark one with each date.)

These folders are where you will put papers that require action but that you don't intend to take care of today. Here are some examples:

- A flier describing your child's class trip that takes place in two days, complete with directions from the school for exactly how their lunches must be bagged, should go in your THIS WEEK file (or, using the expanded tickler file system, in a file for a special date).

- Driving directions to an event you are attending next month belong in the folder for the appropriate month.

- A letter you have written that will require follow-up in a month should go in next month's file.

- A "perfect" birthday card you purchase in April for someone whose birthday is August 15 should go in the August file.

- Reminders to make appointments for your annual physical and six-month dental visit, each occurring at different times of the year, should be placed in the appropriate file for the month when you need to call for the appointment.

step six: say no

I could almost write a complete time management book in two words, and you know what they are—"Say no."

Life today is filled with possibilities. No matter where you live, on any given weekend evening, you could have dinner with friends, go to a movie, attend a live concert or stage play (there are lots of community theaters around), visit a mall with evening hours, play miniature golf at an indoor entertainment center, go bowling, or stay home and rent a DVD or watch TV, surf the Internet, or read a book—and that's only one evening! We are fortunate to have so many choices, but managing all your options means that each person needs to constantly set priorities and then say no to all the rest.

Of course, the choices on weekend evenings are generally about personal preferences. For most of the rest of the week, we have to balance what we have to do, what we ought to do, and what we want to do. We have to make some tough choices regarding responsibility versus personal choice: Do you really need to visit your in-laws every weekend? And will the children survive with a babysitter on a Saturday afternoon so that you can go antiquing? And what about that work you told your boss you'd do on your own time? These choices are tough ones, because they involve what you should do versus what you want to do. Although we all need to be dutiful at work and be good family members and helpful members of our communities, we're no good to anyone if we don't say no now and then so that we can capture some time for ourselves. Burnout is real.

So go back to your time sheet and your priorities list at least once a week and remind yourself, "It really is okay to say no."

step seven: *organize*

No doubt about it, being organized saves time. Again, you'll learn many of my secrets on a subject-by-subject basis as you go through the book. However, for the purposes of this chapter, you just need to know that if you want to find more time for yourself, you need to get and stay organized. Here's why.

Organized people can get things done in less time. The person who is well organized and has a grocery list doesn't need to run back to the store for the ingredient he or she forgot. The person who knows when the car inspection is due doesn't need to call the service station in a panic, trying to get a last-minute appointment. And the person who plans ahead for a party can do a little bit each week, never getting bogged down with a long list of things that have to be done right before the event—or right before the invitations need to be mailed out.

Throughout this book, you'll find lots of advice that will tell you how to get and stay organized—just remember it's worth making the effort to get organized if you're trying to find more time for yourself.

And be realistic. Because staying organized takes time, you'll need to build in time to focus on getting and staying organized (see chapter 2).

step eight: shake things up

You may be thinking that all this stuff about finding more time for yourself sounds very buttoned up, but it's not. The eighth and final step in this chapter is to remind you that we really appreciate our time the most when we do things differently every now and then.

Although you could certainly put the fun back into grocery shopping by taking a friend along or making a scavenger hunt out of it with your kids, most of us simply want to get the must-do items of life out of the way quickly and efficiently—and as pleasantly as possible. Here are some simple ways to make small changes that will let you have a mini-vacation each time you discover something new.

- *Do old activities a new way.* Take a different route home, or, if you live reasonably near work and usually drive, consider riding your bike. Walk the dog at a different time. Go out for dinner on the night you usually order in. Call a friend and meet for a spur-of-the-moment walk. If you usually have dinner with friends on Friday night, have a potluck party with a larger group instead. Take one child away with you for the weekend; let your spouse and the other child find things they want to do.

- *Rekindle old dreams.* If you've always dreamed of being a dancer or playing professional baseball, it may be too late to go pro, but there is no reason not to continue to enjoy the activity. Sign up for a dance class or join a community baseball team.

- *Check your town's cultural listings.* Chances are there is a museum or a performance space you've never visited. Make an effort to do so now.

- *Establish some quiet time that is all your own.* If you have children or work full-time, calling a time-out for thirty minutes to two hours on the weekend is understandably necessary. And whether you nap, read, go for a swim, or take a long walk, that time is yours—so protect it.

- *Treat yourself to a quiet evening in preparation for a good night's sleep.* Now that's a rarity in this day and age!

2

take back your time using a daily planner

To find extra time for yourself, you need to manage the time spent taking care of your regular obligations. Much of this time management relies on having a functional system for keeping track of your schedule.

Whenever clients mention that they have trouble managing their time, I always ask if they have a good calendar system. Because many people have switched from paper to electronic during the past few years, I often hear clients say, "I switched to a computer calendar, but I sometimes forget to enter new information," or "I sometimes forget to check it in the middle of the day."

Sometimes, however, the problem is the number of calendars they keep. It is not uncommon for me to sit down with a client and be shown a personal calendar and a work calendar and then be told about the family calendar at home. This all sounds good, but it is far from a foolproof system. If you have a business breakfast but only refer to your personal calendar at home, how will you know to get up and go to the restaurant instead of to work that day? The only way to function efficiently is to commit to one calendar or planning system that you take with you. If you choose a paper planner or a personal digital assistant, you'll physically carry it with you at all times; if you choose a computer program, you can select systems that you can access from home and from work.

The one exception is the family calendar. The best types of calendars for family management are wall calendars on which the whole family can check at a glance where everyone should be at any given moment. If you have kids and use a family calendar, you just need to coordinate it with your own calendar each night. You don't want to be at work late on the evening that you are supposed to drive the gymnastics car pool.

improving your system

Many people ask me, "Paper or electronic? What's best?" My answer is always the same: "It doesn't matter as long as it works for you."

Today the term *daily planner* is far more appropriate than calendar. An increasing number of people have made the change to computer-based systems, such as handheld electronic devices more commonly known as personal digital assistants (PDAs), and these programs do so much more than keep track of dates.

Don't get me wrong. I'm not antipaper. If you still like a paper-based system, that's workable. I have lots of clients who prefer them. Today's scheduling books also offer many more options. There is plenty of room to note appointments and business expenses. Address books are bound in with the planners, and space is provided for to-do lists where you can set goals, coordinate projects, and keep track of ideas.

Here are a few thoughts on calendar styles. The chapter will conclude with some tips on more effective use of whatever planner you choose.

selecting the planning system that works for you

Investigate paper-based, computer software, and handheld electronic planners and select the one that best suits your lifestyle. Keep in mind the following features:

- Convenience
- Portability
- Cost

- Ease of coordination with spouse, family, or staff members
- Special features you think you would use

handheld electronic devices and computer planners

More and more people are going electronic, and there is a good reason why. Today, most handheld devices actually interface with a computer-based system. If your system is wireless, you can now skip the syncing that used to be necessary to get the two systems to coordinate with each other. You can use your regular computer to input all names and addresses and dates, and then you'll have the data saved in the electronic handheld you carry with you.

The software for these systems usually combines an appointment book, address book, to-do list, and space for other types of notations. Well-designed versions of these systems can be relatively easy to use, and the time management possibilities are amazing.

If you are still trying to decide what type of planner is best for you, consider the following advantages of the electronic systems.

- *Easy rescheduling.* With a few key strokes or a drag-and-drop method, a canceled meeting on Tuesday can be moved to Friday, complete with data on location, telephone number, and driving directions.

- *Scheduling availability at a glance.* If someone calls you to set up an appointment, click on the appropriate icon (symbol) and you'll get a view of your week. Times at which you are already booked show up in a dark color; your available meeting times are shown in white.

- *Dual or group scheduling.* In an office, an assistant and a boss can both input to the same system, making it easy to coordinate schedules and stay up to date. Group scheduling can also be accomplished on a local area network system; a meeting can be entered into everyone's personal planner (although parts of your schedule are public through the system, parts can be kept private, too).

- *Automatic scheduling.* Recurring appointments—for example, a monthly orthodontic appointment for your teen—can be set to appear automatically.

ALLOW EXTRA TIME

To earn a black belt in time management, schedule more time for things than you think you need—for a dentist appointment, this allows time for traffic or for the dentist to run a bit late; for a committee meeting, this allows time to clarify something one-on-one afterward. And if everything runs right on schedule, then you've automatically created extra time for yourself.

- *To-do list carryover features.* "Buy shampoo" will reappear on your list until you have actually taken care of the matter.

- *Search capabilities.* With some programs, you enter what you are looking for—for example, the dental appointment that you prescheduled six months ago—and the computer will help you find the date and time of your next appointment.

- *Space for logs of phone calls and notes.* The latest versions feature "contact manager" functions where notes can be made about a phone conversation you had with someone. When you want to recall what was said, you can pull up the person's name and find a recap of the conversation.

- *E-mail.* Of course, one of the prime attractions of the latest handheld computers is that they receive e-mail. Prices on both the device and the service are dropping.

When shopping for a handheld device, take a good look at the keyboard size and determine whether the screen is easy to read. Some screens are hard to see in certain light. Shop for one that is backlit, and check the screen's visibility in various types of lighting.

paper-based daily planners

Despite the amazing features offered by the latest computerized planners, there are still advantages to using paper-based planners. One of my clients, a very successful real estate agent, still finds that it is easier to have a planner book with her to keep track of everything. "I would never leave the house without it, and because it's 'in my hands' all the time, I never forget to write anything down," she says.

Here are a few of the qualities that have people still happily using paper planners.

- They are portable.
- They are always accessible.
- You don't have to turn it on to access information.
- Data can't be destroyed through an electronic breakdown.
- Your planner is valuable only to you; no one would bother to steal it.
- They can be the least expensive type of calendar planning system.

That said, paper-based systems do lack some of the time-saving elements that computer planners have. One of my favorite elements of computer calendars is the drag and drop feature for rescheduling an appointment. The automatic recurrence of significant personal occasions is also a convenience—once birthdays and anniversaries have been entered, they will pop up year after year.

If you opt for a paper system, evaluate it for portability, be certain there is ample space for each day's appointments, and look for one that has room for a daily to-do list on the same page as your appointment schedule.

the family calendar

Select a large wall calendar (17 × 22 inches is a good size) so that there is space for complete notations about activities. Hang the calendar in a central location near a telephone so that when calls regarding scheduling come in, you can easily check the calendar. Here's how to make this calendar work for your family.

- *Purchase colored pens and assign a different color to each member of the family.* (Select a separate color for activities that involve everyone.) All notations pertaining to that person should be made in the appropriate color. Place a pencil holder nearby for storing the markers, or put them in an easily accessible drawer.
- *Note all significant dates from school calendars as well as after-school, sports, and religious schedules.* That way you will know that

all preplanned activities and events for the year (or the season) are already reflected on the family calendar.

- *Teach children (age seven and older) to take responsibility for their own scheduling.* They can note birthday parties, play dates, and special events they want to attend. (You should supervise younger children to be certain the information is entered correctly, and in the process, you'll be teaching a multitude of helpful lessons—from calendar skills to time management.)

Of course, vital to making a family calendar work is coordinating it with your personal calendar. Therefore, you should check the calendar nightly to see if anything new has been added by another family member. If something has and it will affect you, note it on your personal planner. Similarly, if you make plans at work that affect the family, note it on the family calendar when you get home.

your planner is a priority, so follow these rules

Calendar systems are only as good as the people who use them. I rarely visit clients who have no planner or calendar system at all—they are just misusing the one (or ones!) they have. Here are my planner rules, which will ultimately help free your time by revealing to you the time you do have.

- *Check your planner every day!* You would be surprised at how many people don't do this.

- *Keep your planner easily available.* A readily accessible planner will ensure that you are constantly aware of your schedule.

- *When you set up an appointment, note the address, telephone number, and directions in the space next to the appointment.* That way you will have all the information in one place when you need it.

- *Notate everything, including standing appointments or weekly meetings.* Although you might think you will never forget about the Monday staff meeting, one day you'll be on the phone and someone will say, "How is Monday the fifteenth?" and the next thing you know, you will have accidentally agreed to this conflicting appointment because you had never noted the regularly scheduled meeting.

- *Review your activities a week in advance so that you can plan around existing appointments.* If you have a doctor's appointment in one part of town, you may want to schedule a meeting with a client who is also in that area.

- *Coordinate weekly plans with your partner.* Couples should set aside a few minutes weekly to review upcoming plans and make notations about shared activities or late nights that affect each other. For example, if your spouse is working late one night and you've noted it, you can make plans to see a friend for dinner.

- *Plan weekly meetings to review workplace schedules.* If you need to coordinate your schedule with a boss, a secretary, or a coworker, establish a weekly meeting time to compare schedules and review the week ahead. Be sure to do quick daily checkups so that your workday will go forward as both of you planned.

---

sanity  saver

SCHEDULE IN TIME FOR YOURSELF

Here is the most important planner rule of all: Make appointments with yourself to be certain you have time for your priorities.

If you've ever attended a lecture on financial planning, the number one rule financial planners always recommend is to pay yourself first, meaning that after all your "must pay" expenses such as rent and utilities you should put that leftover money into savings before anything happens to it.

The same is true with finding time for yourself. If you don't protect your own time, everyone around you—family members, coworkers, relatives, and so on—will be happy to help use up all your free time! You need to carefully safeguard the time you want for your own interests. Therefore, whether you block out time for a forty-five-minute morning run or sign up to take a pottery class on the weekend, be sure to note this "self" appointment down on your calendar. Otherwise, you'll soon find that you've let the time get away from you. (See chapter 4 for more suggestions on protecting your time.)

how to handle a crisis

Unfortunately, the best-laid plans are sometimes upset by a family crisis or an emergency. To manage these situations to the best of your ability, take the following steps in advance.

- *Have a list of emergency telephone numbers.* This list should include the contact numbers of relevant family members, your children's schools, medical professionals, and anyone else you might need to reach in case of an emergency.

- *Give trusted neighbors a key to your house.* Don't put your last name or address on the key. If they should lose it or their home is broken into, your key could fall into the wrong hands. Identify it in such a way that you and the neighbor will know that it's your key—for example, by using your pet's name or your nickname.

- *Keep life insurance policies, wills, deeds, and other important documents in a safe-deposit box.* Tell a friend or relative where the key is located.

- *Set up an emergency plan at your place of employment.* Keep a list of your ongoing projects on your computer so that you or someone at the office can quickly access anything that will need to be done if you must be out of the office unexpectedly.

Although we always hope for the best, there might come a time when you are actually faced with a crisis. Use the following tips to help you through the emergency.

- Be prepared to drop many of your responsibilities.

- Realize that it is normal to be exhausted and to feel overwhelmed when trouble hits.

- Be prepared to have food delivered, and don't worry about taking care of the housework.

- Accept help—there will be people offering to do what they can for you. You may be amazed at the wonderful, helpful people you meet when adversity strikes.

- Check in with your boss and find out what is essential. Get coworkers to help out.

■ Do not neglect your own needs. No matter how serious the crisis, a bath, a nap, or some exercise may be just the tonic you need. You're no good to anyone if you are totally stressed out, so build into each day some time for yourself so that you can maintain strength through a difficult period.

your personal address book

If your address book is more than four or five years old, it is probably time to get a new one. People move around so much, and until recently, there was a lot of shifting of cell phone numbers, so if you have a paper-based system, it's probably a mess. To have a complete listing of a contact today, you also need more information than people needed ten years ago. Today, you need a book (or a computer system) that has space for the following:

Name

Home address

Work address

Home phone number

Cell phone number

Office phone number

Personal e-mail address

Work e-mail address

And these items are just the basics—you may also need fax numbers for both home and office and pager numbers.

selecting a new address book or system

The more recent paper-based address books do provide space (although usually tight space) for fax numbers, e-mail addresses, and cell phone numbers in addition to the usual lines for names, street addresses, and telephone numbers. Just be sure you're comfortable with the space allotted.

Another possible solution is a roll file where all names, telephone numbers, and addresses are kept on cards that can be easily snapped in and out. These are simple to update (just create a new card and toss out the old one), and the cards themselves provide adequate space for all the information you need to note about that person. (You can save time by attaching a business card to one of the roll-file cards and writing out any additional information you may need.)

The one big drawback to this system is portability. If you need to carry your address book, this is not the system for you.

Instead, you might prefer a computer solution. If you have not opted for an electronic calendar that will provide you with a portable address book, consider entering your information on your personal computer and creating a printout of the computerized address book. (The printout is for backup purposes; if you have an electronic handheld device that interfaces with your computer, you have the backup you need.) When you buy a program, be sure to check out the search capability—for example, some programs can search for all your friends who live in Indiana. Also ask about print capability if you think you'd like to be able to make a hard copy of your address book at any time.

There are extra advantages to owning a computerized address book.

- *Each entry can be assigned a category.* You may not remember the name of the person who does your picture framing, but requesting a search for "framer" will pull up anyone to whom you have assigned that designation.

- *You can conduct a contact search by location.* If you are going to be in Dallas on business, you can pull up all your contacts in that area.

The biggest drawback to a computer system is the time it takes to enter the names, addresses, and phone numbers. Fortunately, some systems allow you to transfer any information you already have in your computer so that you needn't reenter it. The best way to do the job is by assigning yourself the task of entering a dozen names a day. You can easily accomplish this task in five to ten minutes, and over a period of a few weeks you'll have finished the entire job.

Get in the habit of updating the computer data whenever you receive a change-of-address notification. Print out a backup copy about every six months or so. If you were to have a massive crash of devices, you wouldn't want to lose all your contact information.

3

the amazing power of the to-do list

hen it comes to list making, my clients vary from multi-list people to "what would I do without my BlackBerry?" people to scraps-of-paper people as well as "it's all in my head" people. Although most of my clients swear by "their" method when we first start out, I soon begin to hear tales of woe about what they forgot to do because their system failed them. The stories range from annoying ("I hadn't written it down, so I had to make a second trip to town to pick up my shoes from the repair shop.") to regrettable ("I hadn't made a complete list, and I forgot to send one of my neighbors an invitation to the event.") to the catastrophic ("I'd made the necessary corrections for my boss on a speech he was giving, but we had so much going on I forgot to e-mail it to him. The only copy he had was the uncorrected one, and he was furious.").

Some of my clients have good intentions. They have read about the importance of a to-do list, and they have them—in multiples: a list for work, a list for home, a list of things to pack for vacation, a list of errands for the weekend. One client had so many lists, he had to keep a list of his lists!

Then there are the "scrappers." They use napkins, backs of envelopes, small slips of paper, and Chinese take-out menus to write everything down. Small wonder they are often rummaging through pockets and riffling through papers trying to find the scrap of paper they need.

Second only to your daily planner, the most important tool of time management is having a single, conveniently kept to-do list. With this aid, you can maintain control of your life by keeping track of what needs to be done.

And the best thing is that *writing it down means you don't have to worry about forgetting it.*

creating a new system: your master notebook

The key to life today is to write down *everything* you need to do or keep track of in one long master list. Then keep this list in a notebook to avoid having the "multiple list" problem. And when I speak of creating a master list, I am well aware that most people will need an *office* master notebook and a *personal* master notebook to keep track of two different streams of information. If you're home-based and self-employed, you may be able to rely on a single notebook to serve both purposes. Otherwise, simply pay attention to the advice in this chapter, and re-create another list for the office.

Keep in mind that your list is going to range from entries such as "Buy replacement screen for window" to "Send Mom's birthday card" to "Investigate graduate degree programs"—anything and everything you need to take care of must be written down on the master list.

Some people swear by their computer for list making, but unless you're one of those people whose laptop or handheld electronic device is practically attached to your fingers, I recommend a spiral notebook or a one-inch three-ring notebook system because it's easier to grab and run. Most people feel like kids on the first day of school when I send them to the office supply store to choose a notebook that will be their bible. (And while you are at the office supply store, pick up some appropriate-size subject dividers, which can be enormously handy.) This notebook will absorb all your thoughts and notes. You'll keep a running list of everything you think of, and when you plan out your week you'll sit down with this list to figure out what can be accomplished in the days ahead.

When you have a great idea or a "don't forget" thought while you're in the kitchen or commuting to work, you may still need to make quick notes in a small notebook or even on the always useful scrap of paper. Then you can transfer that task or thought to your master to-do list. That way you'll always have your life under control.

Create a file folder for miscellaneous papers that relate to your master list (label it something like MASTER LIST BACKUP PAPERS). Although you eventually might create a NEW HOUSE file if you're house hunting, when you first begin you may simply have a real estate agent's business card. This master list file is a great place to put this type of item until a full file is warranted.

---

sanity  saver

THE COMPUTERIZED TO-DO LIST

Like the computerized daily planner, a computerized to-do list can do the following.

- Permit you to keep a running record of things you need to do without having to recopy them.
- Integrate the to-do list with your appointment calendar.
- Sort tasks by priority, category, status, or start date.
- Provide you with a neat and legible printout if you prefer to work from a paper to-do list.
- Offer the option of a using it as a family organizer to create to-do lists for various family members.
- Provide alarm reminder options.

If, however, you find that you aren't very conscientious about entering the information on the computer or into your electronic handheld, then there is no shame in sticking with a handwritten to-do list. Some of the most computer-savvy senior executives simply find that handwriting the list makes it more "real" to them.

planning your to-do list for the week

General planning should be done weekly, and it involves working with both your planner and your master notebook. Many people do it on Sunday night. Work-related tasks might be planned on Friday afternoon before leaving the office.

This is your opportunity to take a general look at the week and come to an understanding of what is possible and what isn't. If you have several appointments and an all-day conference one week, this is likely not the time to start a new long-range project. However, if it is a priority item, make a note in your daily planner for the following Monday. Otherwise, these things can slip away from you.

Your daily to-do list should be written in your calendar/planner. If you opted for a computer-based system, add your list to your computer. Next, review your calendar for the upcoming week.

- Do any of your appointments take you to neighborhoods where you can easily accomplish another task from your to-do list? An appointment at the dentist might take you past a store your sister loves. With her birthday coming up, this may be the perfect time to stop in and see if they have an appropriate gift for her.

- Do you need to make special preparations for any of your appointments? Do you need to write these items on your to-do list? If you are not yet finished with a report needed for one of your business appointments, that task will become a priority. Or if this is your week to bring a snack to the T-ball practice, you had better add the items you will need to your grocery list.

- After considering any extra blocks of time you have available, comb through your master notebook. What tasks could you take care of during those blocks of time? Write them down.

- Set priorities based on importance, not urgency, and then take care of these things first. If you start working this way, you will begin to avoid crises because you will have finished what you need to do in advance.

- When you review your master list, take time to write down the steps involved in some of the more complex tasks. While "House hunt" is a huge undertaking, "Call real estate agent," or "Go online to check new listings" are manageable tasks. Interim deadlines on these small steps can keep your project moving forward.

■ *Don't overschedule.* Write down what you conservatively feel you will be able to accomplish—a couple of larger priority items and perhaps three or four other items on a list are generally what most people can expect to accomplish each day. That way you won't feel overwhelmed, and you will have a feeling of accomplishment at being able to do what you set out to do for the day.

■ *Group similar activities so that you can complete the tasks in an organized fashion.* For example, if you are going to the mall, scan through your list and note everything that you need to do while there—and there may be a convenient stop or two on the way to the mall, so write those errands down, too. This principle also pertains to desk-related tasks. If you need to write five business e-mails or three thank-you notes, take care of them all at the same time.

■ *Set appointments with yourself.* If you want to write the Great American Novel or finally master that computer program you've been intending to investigate, figure out how much time you can devote to it each week and write it down as an unbreakable appointment. These appointments can also be used for simply taking a walk. You bought this book for a reason, and I'm here to give you permission to set yourself and your activities as a new priority.

identify your personal prime time

Every person has a metabolic high period during the day when he or she has more energy. By early adulthood most of us know whether we are morning people or night owls. Scheduling priority tasks during this peak time is the key to doing your best work most efficiently. Your thoughts will be clearer, and you will be able to execute them more rapidly.

If you're not sure when you're at your best, consider the following traits:

Morning people

Get up early even on the weekends

Enjoy getting a lot accomplished early in the day

sanity saver

YOUR "PRIME TIME" SHOULD BE RESERVED FOR PRIORITIES

We all have priorities, and we all have an ideal time when we're at our best for dealing with them. If you want to find extra time for yourself, it is important to respect this fact, and take care of what you need to at the time that is best for you. Do you know when your prime time is?

When you think about setting aside prime time for yourself, remember that real life happens. Take into account your family situation and the interruptions that are almost always inevitable. You may need to wake up thirty minutes early or to book child care for Saturday mornings if you can't find other time when you won't be interrupted.

It is also important that you don't procrastinate after setting aside some prime time for yourself. (Chapter 5 offers tips on overcoming the urge to procrastinate.)

Exercise early rather than late

Don't really like staying out late

Fall asleep during the late-night news

Night people

Have trouble waking up in the morning

Get into better moods as the day goes on

Prefer to exercise at the end of the day

Like afternoons or evenings better than mornings

Find it easy to read late into the night

If you still aren't certain when your prime time is, try doing two similar crossword puzzles, but tackle them at two different times of day. Did you do best on the morning one, or the one you did in the afternoon? The one you found easiest to do and did most quickly likely reflects your best time for dedicated work.

Depending on how you identify yourself, you should use your own prime time for your most difficult task of the day. At the office, it may be writing up a report. At home, it might be organizing your financial documents for a tax preparer or coming up with a plan for a fund-raiser you promised to organize.

- If you are a morning person, start on your task as one of the day's first undertakings. If you are a night owl who has to get up anyway, do low-level tasks until you are fully functioning, and then dive into the task at hand. (Owls should still try to get to their priorities as early as possible. As the day grows older, there is an increase in occurrences that will interfere with your prime time.)

- Set a specific start time, or the day will get away from you.

- Don't waste your prime time. One client, a real early bird, used her precious morning hours at the office to return routine phone calls and finish with mail from the day before. After our consultation she realized how important it was to do those things in the afternoon, using her mornings for major tasks that required concentration.

- If you must keep working past your peak productivity time, take a break and do something invigorating like walking around the block or phoning a friend who always makes you laugh. You will return to the task feeling refreshed and energetic enough to see it through to completion.

the nightly update

A weekly planning session gives you a general idea of what the week holds. On a nightly basis you need to update the plan for the next day. And by creating this list the night before, you are able to get up in the morning and make a fresh run at the list. Here are some other reminders.

- You may discover that an unexpected occurrence prevented you from accomplishing the tasks you intended to do one day, so those items must be moved forward to another day.

■ Your boss has requested something, adding a new priority to your week, so you will need to juggle your day to accommodate this addition.

■ An appointment may be canceled, providing you with the perfect block of time to finish something old or start something new.

■ After you've created your daily list, number the items by order of priority. This provides you with an order of attack.

■ As you complete tasks, they should be crossed off both your master notebook list and the daily to-do list in your planner.

■ Unfinished tasks should be moved forward. If something is being carried over for too long, reevaluate the task. There may be a reason why it is not getting done.

■ Gather contact names, phone numbers, and other materials you expect to need for the next day's projects before you go home at night. That way you can get a running start the next morning.

sample lists

Here are some sample lists that may be inspirational.

general lists

The asterisk indicates a priority for that day. Remember that only two to three items can realistically be thought of as priorities.

Monday To-Do List

Finish running numbers for next year's budget; to Harry by 5 P.M.

Investigate what is expected for my speech at next month's conference

Follow up with Sue on Smith account

Call personnel and be sure paperwork is under way for new hire

Ask Mary to look into airline schedule for next month's conference

Phone to reschedule dentist appointment

On the Way Home

Buy lettuce, red pepper, bananas

Pick up prescriptions

In the meantime, this person may have an ongoing weekend to-do list similar to the following:

Errands

Stop at farmers' market

Grocery

Dry cleaner's

Shoes to shoemaker

Birthday gift for Sylvia

Buy wrapping paper

Call June, Ann, Michele, Tom, and Fred about organizing neighborhood meeting re: zoning change

Catch up with weeding

Prepare lasagna for later in the week

Pre-pack the nonperishable parts of lunch

task-specific lists

The parent who is considering sending a child to sleepaway camp for the first time might have a list with these items:

Investigating Sleepaway Camps

Call camp-finder rep that Mary used—get recommendations

Call Jerry to get the name of the camp his kids attend

Do an Internet search for likely places

Investigate locations and consider visiting a few of them?

Questions to ask the camp:

- Can you tell me about your program?
- What kind of experience/background do your counselors have?
- Do you have a full-time camp nurse?
- Do lots of first-timers attend this camp?
- How do you deal with homesickness?

And, of course, the more you become involved in the process, the longer your to-do list will become.

For the person planning a weekend getaway, there would likely be two lists that should be created early in the week.

Before the Trip

Ask neighbor to hold newspaper and set of keys

Wash T-shirts

Iron khaki pants

Pick up pink sweater from cleaners

Try on bathing suits

Buy hostess gift

Take dogs to pet sitter

Toss out food that will spoil

Turn off air conditioners

Leave one light on

Packing List

check that toiletry bag is complete

books

glasses, sunglasses

suntan lotion

meds, vitamins

house keys

health bars

3 T-shirts (white, black, pink)

khaki pants

white pants

wrap skirt

pink sweater

flats

walking shoes

belt

tennis outfit, tennis shoes, hat, and racket

sleepwear (gown, robe—can wear flats for slippers)

bathing suit and cover-up

avoiding waiting time

No doubt about it—the best way to get a lot of things done is by doing them when no one else is around. That way you avoid lines and avoid waiting. A study by the Fortino Group in Pittsburgh found that over the course of a lifetime the average person spends *five years* waiting in line. While you can always take along reading material or have an audiobook loaded into your MP3 player for times when you must wait, it's best to try to avoid waiting if you can. For the most part, lines are usually shortest midweek and early in the day. Here are some other tips on how to avoid waiting.

- *Plan in advance.* Movies, museums, and other tourist attractions often allow you to buy tickets by phone, specifying the date and arrival time. At amusement parks you can sometimes get a ticket ahead of time for certain rides.

- *Learn to calculate waiting time.* In a grocery store, for example, the lengthiest lines are often at registers the farthest away from the store's entrance, because most people shop in a circle.

- *Always have something with you (such as reading materials or a small notebook for jotting things down) in case you do have to wait.*

- *Always have a map in the car (or use your navigation system) for when you are stuck in traffic.* If you know the back roads, you may be able to find a way out of a traffic jam. Traffic reports on the radio can be helpful in assessing whether it's worth looking for an alternative route or whether the road opens up in a mile or two, and it isn't worth the bother. If you anticipate that you may hit bad traffic before you leave home or the office, go online and search for traffic reports and Web cams. This will give you an opportunity to switch routes if you decide it's necessary.

Here are some additional time-saving strategies.

- *Prescriptions:* Try to avoid Mondays and Fridays as well as the days before and after a holiday. These are often the heaviest periods of calls and visits to doctors, so pharmacists tend to be particularly busy at that time.

- *Supermarket:* The quietest times at the supermarket are usually anytime before 3 P.M. on Tuesdays and Fridays. Most days before 9 A.M. and most evenings after 7 P.M. are also a little calmer, so you can slip in then and beat the rush.

- *Mailing packages:* Although it may seem counterintuitive to go at lunchtime, most post offices have additional personnel assigned to window duty during lunch hour, so the post office lines move more quickly than at other times of the day. Also keep your eyes peeled for satellite postal stations. In major cities, a post office "sales" truck will sometimes park on a busy street corner, and people can mail packages and pick up stamps from this mobile sales window. If your post office waits seem to take an eternity, however, you may want to explore one of the package service storefronts that have sprung up in the last few years. They generally ship with several different services so they can price shop for you and most also sell stamps as a customer courtesy. They will also store frequently used addresses in their computer for you, which saves time when you drop off packages.

- *Gas or auto repair work:* Aim for midweek. Mondays and Fridays are particularly bad for getting these things done.

- *Doctors, dentists:* Request the first appointment of the day, except on Mondays. (Doctors are generally catching up with cases from the weekend early on Monday mornings.)

- *Airports:* Print your boarding pass at home or use the self-check-in kiosks at the airport.

4

how to get things
done and still have
time for yourself

*I*f time management were easy, people wouldn't need consultants like me. We are all human, and if left to our own preferences, we would all choose to do:

- A task we enjoy over one we don't enjoy—for example, planting new seedlings would usually trump weeding

- A simple task (cleaning out the snack drawer in the kitchen) versus a hard or time-consuming one (cleaning the entire basement or clearing out old files that need to be read through for possible items to save)

- A task that brings an immediate reward (if I return this phone call, I can cross it off my list) versus one with delayed gratification (I need to work really hard on this consumer analysis report that is due in two weeks)

- The familiar (having your regular crowd in for Sunday brunch) versus the new (having coworkers you just met over for dinner)

■ A task with a guarantee (that committee always does a great job, and it's a fun group of people) versus something with a questionable outcome (this new committee has to be built from scratch)

This chapter will strengthen your ability to implement the suggestions in chapters 1 through 3 to get the must-do items in your life—including time just for you—taken care of. It is not that difficult, but it does mean dedicating yourself to working toward managing your time every single day.

staying focused on priorities

Within your master notebook (or your computerized to-do list), there are many types of tasks, but some are much more important than others. Scan through the items you've listed.

At home, the most important tasks are generally dictated by upcoming events. If you are having company for dinner, then cooking is a top priority. If the clothes dryer is on the blink, either getting it repaired or shopping for a new one must be accomplished. If you are leaving on a business trip tomorrow, packing is your number one activity.

You should also have in mind long-term priorities. Tasks such as shopping in advance for the holidays, getting the air conditioner checked before the weather warms up, and getting the roof repaired are important. By accomplishing these tasks in an orderly manner, you reduce the potential crises that may necessitate taking a day off from work or canceling out of something fun because your refrigerator died on you or the roof leak became so bad that one of your rooms flooded.

At work, your top priorities should be those that lead to more productivity or to higher sales—something that contributes to the success of the company. Keeping up with day-to-day tasks like taking phone calls or processing the mail must be done at some point, but these tasks should not occupy prime time because they are not your top priorities.

As you go through your master notebook, put a red asterisk next to items that take priority. This notation will remind you to put them on your daily to-do list as soon as possible.

As for your daily list, each item you select to complete on a given day should be ranked in order of priority. In general, you should expect to work on no more than two top-priority items per day. You will run out of either time or energy before you can tackle more. The other items on your to-do list should be more basic projects that do not require a big block of time or a high level of concentration.

"everything is a top priority!"

I hear this cry from clients all the time. But the reality is that not everything has the same importance. If you are unable to distinguish what your current priorities are, here is what to do.

- Ask yourself, "What really must be done today—and what can wait?"

- If you look at your list for the day and find that there are more than two main projects and six to eight smaller items on it, then it's too long. Reevaluate the items listed and consider the consequences of the delay: Your boss won't have what he needs for his presentation if you don't finish the research, so that's a top priority. The salesperson who wants to meet with you—and who seems to have a good idea—is a priority, but how about rescheduling him? He really doesn't have to be seen today. At home, the we're-out-of-milk errand needs to be done; the gift you plan to return could be brought back on the weekend. This process of reexamining your list should pare your list down to a more manageable number.

- The items that have to be dropped from today's priority list should be rescheduled for a specific day. This helps you avoid a last-minute panic over whatever those tasks entailed.

If you are still having difficulty establishing your priorities, discuss with someone what you think is most important. At work, a fellow employee can be a good sounding board; at home, a spouse or a good friend can be helpful. (When I am contacted by clients, I frequently serve this purpose. They need someone objective to help them see their way out of an unproductive cycle.)

flexibility and your priorities

Once you've deemed something a priority, it would be nice if you could just get it done and not think about it again.

When I work with clients, I show them that priority setting must be done constantly. Along with death and taxes, change is another thing that is guaranteed in life. Our world is constantly shifting, so to make the best use of our time, we need to be prepared to manage what comes our way. If your boss arrives in your office with a new assignment and tells you to temporarily set aside the prep work you're doing for next month's big sales conference, here are the three steps you should take.

1. Shift to the most-pressing priority.

2. Gather all the materials pertaining to the project you were working on and make notes about where you were on the project. By organizing your background information, you can pick up right where you left off when you return to the project.

3. Reschedule a time for the work that had been your priority.

Too often people miss the second and third steps. A higher-priority item comes up and they respond to it. They abandon their current project without even putting away the materials. As a result, people can lose data.

At home, shifting priorities can be equally difficult, largely because these priorities often involve a high level of emotion. You may have promised to take your eleven-year-old on an outing, but when her two-year-old brother develops a high fever, you're faced with little choice—the needs of the sick child predominate.

Some people become "undone" about a scheduling change and are annoyed because "I had it all planned out so that I could finish my work and then . . . crisis hit." Although it is vexing to have to switch plans, flexibility—bouncing back—actually saves time. Becoming angry just wastes more time. Instead of focusing on the unpredictability of your circumstances, focus on the outcome you need to achieve from the cards that have been dealt you.

priorities rule! (rules for priorities)

Here are the five things you need to remember about priorities. And remember, a priority can be a work-related task, a family obligation, or the time you've set aside just for you.

1. A priority is something you do first, not last.

2. Always keep your own priorities foremost in your mind.

3. If your priority conflicts with someone else's, consider whose needs must come first. If it's your boss, you may need to take care of that issue before the others, and then address your own priorities. If the conflict is with another family member or a colleague, talk to the other person and see if a compromise can be worked out.

4. Acknowledge that priorities can change because of time constraints and situations beyond your control.

5. Don't let interruptions or the frivolous demands of others keep you from achieving your goals.

make yourself a priority

My clients all have the same types of complaints. They tell me: "The phone rings; someone drops in with a question; some minor occurrence creates an emergency I have to handle. I never have time to work on what is really important!" The answer is to take care of yourself first.

At the beginning of the week when you plan out your schedule and select what projects you would like to undertake, make an appointment with yourself. If you know that every morning from 8:00 to 8:45 A.M. is to be devoted to something that is important to you, you will find that you will automatically preserve this time. Because you've selected a specific time slot, you are less likely to forget and schedule something at that time. (Write it on your calendar anyway—then when you're flustered and trying to work in an appointment based on someone else's schedule, you'll still have the written reminder that a certain time is scheduled to be yours.)

You may need to be creative to carve out this special time for yourself at work. Consider going to the office earlier in the morning when things are still quiet. Some businesspeople do the reverse: they stay at home later doing work that requires concentration or returning important phone calls. "Then when I get to the office, I am available for all the crises that are destined to occur that day," says a retail executive whose children are grown. "I have done some of the work that is most important to me, so I am ready to cope with what is new." To work productively, some people find it helpful to remove themselves from their normal environment. They go to the library, to a conference room at the office, or to a neighborhood coffee shop where they can work uninterrupted for the allotted time.

If a set appointment (same time each day) is unthinkable because of your schedule, then scan your week. How many days can you schedule even twenty minutes for yourself? Block those times in by writing them down in your calendar as if they were medical appointments. That way you won't even think of breaking your appointment with yourself!

Get into the habit of finding time for yourself every week. You will soon feel more in control because the work that is important to you will be getting done. That will be a very satisfying feeling.

looking for more time

Most of my clients find that they still need more time. And the situation seems to be getting worse, not better. When I first started my business, I was usually retained to help with organizational issues; today, most people call because they are desperate to find more time in their hectic schedules. Here is what I tell them.

You can add hours to your day by getting up a little earlier. When you read interviews with novelists, a large number of them write in the early mornings before leaving home to go to nine-to-five jobs. That's good time management! They found time for doing something that was very important to them. Other people use those early morning hours to have some time to exercise, to read the newspaper, or even to get laundry done before the rest of the household is up. That time is theirs, and they would be lost without it.

How much earlier should you arise? I personally find that an extra thirty minutes can make a difference in your day. Consider your current waking time and your current bedtime. Based on this, how many hours of sleep do you seem to need? The trick is to choose a time that is early enough to give you a few extra minutes but not so early that you find yourself sleep-deprived.

To maximize your own time by getting up a little earlier, you may find that you need to go to bed a little earlier. Most of us drift through the evening, reading or watching television and staying up "just a little longer." If you make an effort to capture a little more sleep time at night, the chances are good that you won't really miss much. (If you have a favorite television program that ends late in the evening, record it to watch at a different time during the week.)

Additional motivation for getting up early may be provided by planning to do something specific at that time. Whether it is going for a walk, taking up a new hobby, or getting to the gym before work, select something specific that you want to do. This will undoubtedly make it easier to remain committed to your goal.

One final bit of advice: do your best to maintain a weekend sleep schedule that is relatively close to your weekday hours. Scientific studies of body rhythms have shown that people function better

> quick **GO!** start
> ## DO IT NOW
> "Do it now" whenever you can.
>
> If you take something off or out, or put something down, put it away as soon as you're finished with it. File meeting-related papers as soon as the meeting is over. Send your RSVP to invitations as they arrive. Unpack parcels and groceries as soon as you get home. Do whatever you can to minimize creating a backlog of things to do.

when they sleep and wake at regular times seven days per week. An added benefit is that a weekend morning is a wonderful time to use for something just for you.

haste makes waste

Can you think of a time when you had to hurry to complete something and suffered that harried, unable-to-concentrate feeling of rushing and just wanting it done? Once you devote the time to a project, it is important to concentrate fully on the task and to work carefully and methodically. Transposed numbers or carelessly written sentences will create trouble—and cost time—later on, so work at a pace where you are relatively certain you won't make a mistake.

If you have set aside the time for the project and have scheduled in time for the other important projects you need to do that day, you don't need to rush.

time ⏱ booster

FINISH WHAT YOU CAN AS YOU GO ALONG—WHAT IS LEFT UNDONE ALL TOO OFTEN REMAINS UNDONE

I often come in contact with my client's true habits. I get to see the boxes and bags that are hidden before visitors arrive. I hear tales of why my clients just can't get anything done.

Almost everyone hates finishing the same things. In my experience, filing is the number one hated task at the office; around homes, people complain of unsorted paperwork and photographs that will probably never make it into an album. (Digital photographs are beginning to change this gripe, however.)

Don't leave household tasks undone. Make your bed first thing in the morning. Do the dishes right after a meal. Take a damp paper towel (keep a roll under the bathroom sink) and wipe up after you have washed in the morning.

Avoid putting off until tomorrow everything from a phone call to a basket of laundry, a pack of reading material to yesterday's mail. If you take care of things as you go along, you won't have to make time to go back and pick up. These new habits will permit you to get things done before the tasks ever need to go on a list.

Many people have problems finishing what they start. Here are ten quick tips to make sure you get things done.

1. Keep a clean desk or work area. Starting out with a neat desk each day means that you don't have yesterday's pile of paperwork to comb through, and your outlook will be brighter knowing that you are making a fresh start.

2. Be selective about the responsibilities you agree to take on.

3. Write down things you need to do. Successful people are habitual about keeping a running list of tasks.

4. Don't clog your brain by trying to remember conversations and project details. If you are having ongoing discussions with

someone about a certain issue, write down pertinent notes in your master notebook or your computerized contact manager. When the discussion resumes, you will have a complete account of what has been agreed so far.

5. If your office has a voice-mail system, it can be a great get-it-done method for leaving messages to yourself. No matter the time of day, simply pick up the phone and record your message. The reminder will be waiting for you when you are ready to retrieve it.

6. Make it easy on yourself by establishing a pleasant environment for a disliked task. If you hate paying bills, plan to do it while listening to your favorite music or watching a DVD.

7. When conducting research, don't hold out for that last statistic or that one last bit of information. You may wait forever, and sometimes it's more important just to be done. Determine a time when you will move ahead with the research you have. As you work, you will either determine that the additional data isn't necessary or you'll increase the pressure on the person who needs to help you get it.

8. Be decisive. Most day-to-day decisions should be made quickly. At the office, make decisions on everything that you can. The same is true at home. Yes or no to attending the Joneses' barbecue? Yes or no to the letter from the local wildlife preserve asking for money? The longer you wait to make up your mind on something, the more time and energy this consumes.

9. Delegate what you can.

10. If the task is burdensome, plan on a reward for completing it. Small rewards like going to the movies with a friend can be put in place for interim deadlines. For larger accomplishments, consider promising yourself an evening out or a massage, which can make the effort necessary seem worthwhile.

getting things done

Today's culture actually makes it difficult to get things done, as my clients complain to me constantly, and I can only agree. The interruptions to our time are constant and the number of things demanding our attention is unprecedented.

Clients tell me they constantly feel overwhelmed. I think of this as the Ping-Pong effect on life. Your mind jumps from task to task, and your eye wanders from pile to pile of paperwork. It becomes almost impossible to get things done.

Another problem we all face is being realistic about what we actually can accomplish. I visit executives with twenty must-do items on their to-do list to accomplish in a single day. Even on a perfect day, with no interruptions or anything unexpected occurring, this would be a difficult feat. On a normal day, it is impossible.

So here are a few more techniques that will help you work on what you *need* to get done, so that you'll be able to find time for what you *want* to get done.

break big projects down into small steps

Dividing a project into manageable parts is the first step in any type of task management. This process makes the overall project more comprehensible, while it provides you with a blueprint of exactly what must be done.

If you have ever asked a child to clean up his or her room, you quickly learn this request is ineffective. Yet if you say to a toddler, "Please put your blocks away," or to a teen, "Hang up all the clothes on your floor, please, and empty your wastebasket," you have provided specific, manageable tasks. The tools are clear (the toddler will need a container for the blocks; the teen will need hangers for the clothes and a garbage bag for the trash), and the exact expectations have been presented.

As adults we must perform this request clarification for ourselves. What does it really mean to be asked to be a trustee for an estate, or to be chairperson of a committee? And while something like preparing a speech, writing a report, or decorating for the holidays sounds relatively clear, it is only because these tasks are a little more familiar to us. Each one still needs to be broken down into a few steps that can be accomplished in twenty- to -sixty-minute blocks of time, because realistically most of our lives must be lived in these smaller segments. (When was the last time you had a totally free afternoon?)

The benefits of preparation are obvious when you watch any of the cooking, crafting, or home-building programs on television. Hosts of these shows accomplish large and overwhelming projects—from preparing a Thanksgiving feast to building a patio—by breaking the project down into small steps. (Of course, they have the advantage of a staff to help get the job done—a reminder to all of us that it's okay to ask for help when we need it.)

Selling your house is a good example of an overwhelming task that can be organized into many parts. From scanning newspaper ads and the Internet to get general ideas of prices to calling a couple of real estate agents for appraisals, there are many tasks to take care of on the way to a successful sale. As you come closer to putting the house on the market, you will find that you face a growing list of to-do items, but they can still be written down as relatively small steps. (For example, "fluffing" your house—making it as presentable as possible in preparation for selling it—can be written down as a room-by-room to-do list.)

With practice, breaking down smaller tasks like "Clean out files" or "Sort through photographs" or "Reseed lawn" will become second nature to you. This experience will polish your skills for approaching the larger, more overwhelming tasks that we all face. Keep in mind that any task, no matter how large, remains achievable if you take it one step at a time.

find step one

So how do you identify step one? For most people, the first step relies on personal priorities, and your top priority becomes the point from which every other step will follow in a timely and orderly way.

Think through the project before you, and select where you want to start. Perhaps you want to improve the appearance of your yard. Think about what part of your yard bothers you most. Is it the area you see when you drive up to the house, or would you like a more beautiful scene when you sit on the back deck in the evening? Step one should address the area that is your top priority.

Some tasks are going to require input from other people. For example, at the office you may need to assemble some type of report, but you need input from others before you can get the job done. Therefore, step one should be calling a meeting of those people who must contribute information for the report.

If the task is something like cleaning out the basement, choose what is bothering you the most and start there. Or if your motivation for focusing on the basement is that your neighborhood is having a group tag sale, start by going through your belongings looking for what you want to sell. This will almost certainly make the basement look better right away.

if you are struggling with the first step, start in the middle

I find that sometimes clients know very well what the first step of a project is—they just don't want to do it. This is when I counsel that they should start in the middle, choosing a part of the process with which they feel comfortable or about which they feel passionate. If I can get someone speaking excitedly about what it is he or she is supposed to do, it will quickly become clear to both the client and myself where it is best to begin. On your own, try to think about the easiest way to slip into the project.

One client of mine was unhappy because he had to give a marketing presentation at a big meeting. Because he didn't like public speaking, he didn't want to write the speech. After working with him for a while, I discovered that he was a "numbers" guy. He became very animated when showing me charts and graphs of the progress they were making and the plans they had. Surprisingly, he was also pretty good at explaining what he was showing. I counseled him to "jump into the middle," by preparing the section of the PowerPoint presentation that involved his charts and graphs, which of course was also the "meat" of the talk. I told him the introduction would write itself if he did this important step first.

About six weeks later, he called to tell me that the presentation had been very well received.

Whether you start your project at step one or smack-dab in the middle, here are some guidelines to accomplish things more efficiently.

- *Take time to plan the steps in your undertaking.* Note if any of the steps must be done in a particular order.

■ *Set a manageable and realistic goal.* By establishing achievable goals, you will be inspired to keep working because you will see that the task can be completed. If you are cleaning out the attic, you aren't likely to finish in a single afternoon, but it is reasonable to expect to finish reorganizing one set of shelves. Novelists often promise themselves that they will write five pages per day, and though it may take months to finish an entire book, each day they can enjoy a feeling of accomplishment for having met their pages-per-day quota.

■ *Create deadlines and interim checkpoints.* You must finish the special report for work in two weeks. Your goal for the attic clean-out may be to get it done within two months, with parts of the project accomplished along the way. Whatever the project, note down interim deadlines for each step so that you will know if you are running ahead or falling behind.

■ *Block out the time to accomplish what you need to do.* Little tasks can be slotted into odd moments of a day; major tasks require setting aside bigger blocks of time. Whether it is rewriting your résumé or cleaning out a closet, you need to set aside time to work on the project. Even twenty to thirty minutes of uninterrupted time can make all the difference. You will also find that by establishing a set period

mini vacation

USE THOSE SPARE MOMENTS WISELY

What do you do when you catch a spare minute after working on a specific project?

What you *need* to do is give yourself a mini-vacation. If you've been working alone, call a friend. If you've been working as part of a committee, then go out and take a stroll by yourself, or suggest a group lunch to celebrate. To function effectively, your body craves change, so do something that loosens up your muscles and gives your brain a break. You'll be able to concentrate better once you've done something else for a short time.

of time in which to do a project, you will be more efficient. If you give yourself a full afternoon to finish a one-hour task, for example, you'll find that the job will expand unnecessarily to fill the time.

■ *Create the right environment.* Put a sign on your door that reads DO NOT DISTURB, and let the phone go to voice mail for a specified period of time. Or take your laptop with you to the library or the coffee shop where you can find the mental peace you need.

■ *Make it convenient to do what you need to do.* Before you begin, make certain you have what you need for the project. Arrange to have the tools and materials you need placed conveniently nearby. If you need to wrap gifts for the holidays, doing so is much easier and quicker if you have a place where you can spread out the proper supplies. Too often people start a task and then find that they have to keep hopping up and down to get the things they need. If you are working on your taxes, you will need your financial records, a calculator and/or the computer program with your financial data on it, and all the appropriate tax forms. If you are answering formal letters for work, be sure to have letterhead, envelopes, stamps (for a home office), and any additional papers you need. If you are hanging pictures at home, make certain you have the right hooks or nails and wire. Gather your supplies first, even if that means a trip to the store to purchase them, before you start your project.

■ *Learn to delegate.* At the office, delegate any part of the project you can; if it's a household chore, ask other family members to help out.

■ *Give the task your full attention.* Full concentration is the key to getting things done. Whether it is cooking a meal or writing a lengthy business letter, the project will be completed more quickly if you focus fully.

■ *Clean up when finished.* Although leaving a project out on your desk or spread out on a table for the next day may seem like a good idea at the time, a clean work area is far more inspiring than one where you have to reassess where you were when you left off. Make a rule that when your work time on a particular project ends, pack up the project neatly and put it away. That way you can start fresh on whatever you need to the next day.

5

overcoming the three thieves: lateness, interruptions, and procrastination

When I consult with clients in their homes and offices, I find that three thieves of time recur with maddening frequency: lateness (both yours and someone else's), interruptions, and procrastination.

In my mind, the word *lateness* conjures up my sister Jane. I love her dearly, but promptness is not her strong suit. I used to say that Jane would be late to her own wedding. Then she was—and almost missed her honeymoon flight, too. Recently, I've acquired a new Jane story. She and her husband were coming to my town to participate in a religious ceremony for my twins. The service started—no Jane. I was beside myself worrying about what to do, who would step in, how I would explain in the middle of the service that they weren't there . . . then at just the moment that their names were called, they walked in. (What timing!) We can laugh about it now, but sometimes I still feel myself becoming annoyed all over again.

So if you want to find more time for yourself—and not annoy your big sister or anyone else—you can use this chapter as a blueprint for overcoming these time management hurdles (lateness, interruptions, and procrastination).

the first thief: lateness—
yours and someone else's

While other people's lateness is an obvious time-waster for you, believe it or not, your own lateness is a time waster as well. When clients describe being halfway to the airport and realizing they don't have their driver's license for identification, or when they talk about being so stressed before a presentation that they rushed through it and made mistakes, the stories they tell me are usually preceded by a tale of how they were running so late in the morning that they forgot something, or they were so breathless they couldn't collect their thoughts. Trust me, if you want to find time for yourself, creating a more orderly life is part of the process. And once you feel calmer and more collected, you'll soon find you can get out of the house on time and be in control of what you need for the day. It's a much better feeling!

making promptness a priority

Even if other people are late, you will be best served by making promptness a priority. If you are organized and well prepared, your stress level will go down, thereby making extra moments available to you for what *you* choose to do. For example, if you are meeting a chronically late friend for lunch, don't make yourself crazy trying to figure out ways to be as late as he or she is. Instead, arrive on time but take along something you've been wanting to do, such as a new crossword puzzle or a magazine you haven't had time to read. You can create a mini-vacation while sitting comfortably at the restaurant where you agreed to meet.

There is a wonderful story about promptness and the great Russian composer Tchaikovsky. A lady asked him where he got his inspiration, and he is supposed to have said, "Madam, when I walk into my studio every morning at 8 A.M., the muses had better be on time."

So here's to being on time!

managing morning departures

Morning is by far the most challenging time of day to be on time. Parents are usually leaving with children—or leaving children behind, which can be equally difficult. Yet for single people, a morning departure can still be a struggle.

A couple years ago, the *New York Times* solicited readers' tales of reasons why they arrived at work late. Although the stories included all the standard ones—bad weather, balky kids, and car trouble—there were two that particularly caught my attention: "My favorite actress just got married—I needed time alone" and "My husband's pet spider died, and I had to console him."

So you see, it doesn't take much to slow us down in the morning.

The secret to a good morning is to prepare as much as you can the night before. As I like to say: Start the day right . . . at night.

- Parents are told to have children select their clothing the night before, and adults should do this, too. By making your what-to-wear decision in the evening, you will spend less time getting dressed in the morning. If the weather changes unexpectedly, you'll find that modifying an outfit (warmer top or different shoes) is easier than selecting an outfit from scratch.

- Your purse or briefcase should also be packed the night before. That way you've made all the what-do-I-need-tomorrow decisions when your thoughts were clearer than in the grogginess of morning awakening.

- Teach children to put completed homework in their backpacks as soon as they are finished.

- Have family members line up backpacks and briefcases by the door.

- Make lunches immediately after dinner.

- If you can't finish everything the night before, leave yourself a note on the kitchen counter to remind you of what needs to be taken care of the next morning.

In the morning make sure you do the following.

- Make your bed as soon as you get up.

- Try to finish each group of tasks as you go. Don't hop from room to room as you are getting ready. When you go to the kitchen for breakfast, fix it, eat it, and clean up before leaving the room. And work neatly. In the bathroom, put the cap back on the toothpaste and wipe the sink—it takes only a few seconds—so you won't have cleanup to do later on.

- Avoid using multiple personal-care products. Women can reduce getting-ready time by visiting a department store makeup counter for easy-to-use products that do double duty: look for moisturizers with sunblock and easy-on makeup sticks that contain cover-up and promise a dry, satiny finish so no powder is needed.

- Keep clocks in both the bathroom and the bedroom so that you can keep track of the time while you're getting ready.

- Call to confirm appointments before you leave home. You may discover that the person with whom you have an appointment is out sick that day. If you learn that the doctor or dentist is running late with appointments, you can plan accordingly.

beating chronic lateness

For some of us, punctuality is an elusive goal despite our best intentions. If you chronically have trouble getting to places on time, here are some remedies.

- Be sure you have a clock in every room—even the bathroom.

- Set your clocks a few minutes ahead.

- In your calendar, mark your appointments earlier than they really are.

- Keep a kitchen timer in the bathroom and keep setting it for ten-minute intervals to remind yourself to keep going.

the second thief: interruptions and how to reduce them

Interruptions are the number one obstacle we face when it comes to controlling our time. The delivery person needs your signature during dinner; your cell phone rings just as you are putting the baby down for a nap; and the dog escapes from the yard when you are about to leave the house for a doctor's appointment. At the office it only gets worse. The calls never stop, the influx of e-mail is daunting, and in all likelihood, you have lots of people around you, meaning that an ever-increasing group may come by your desk to ask for something, tell you something, or simply stop to visit.

Whether you are at home or at work, unremitting interruptions are stressful—your brain overloads trying to process what you *want* it to concentrate on versus what is happening around you.

What to do? Stand up for yourself. If you don't step in and begin to control as many interruptions as you can, you'll never be able to have the focused time you need and deserve. To minimize interruptions, I teach a two-step plan:

1. Anticipate interruptions so that you can reduce or manage them.

2. Shorten those interruptions that occur.

anticipating interruptions

Many interruptions that occur are ones you could have foreseen. For example, at work, a newly hired employee is likely to have questions, and at home at dinnertime, your children may need help with homework. These interruptions are far less annoying if you make time allowances for them. Here are some ideas for coping.

- *Be realistic about how much time you can preserve as uninterrupted time.* Most people can probably protect only about an hour of their time, although some may be lucky enough to set aside as many as three hours. If you accept that you have to be open to interruptions at some point, it may be easier to protect the small amount of time you are trying to claim as your own.

- *Group interruptions that you can foresee.* At work, schedule all your appointments during a block of time in the morning or afternoon. At home, try to arrange that the sofa you ordered will be delivered on the same day that the dryer repairman has agreed to come.

- *Seem less available than you are to reduce the likelihood of being someone's first choice for help or for socializing.* At the office, angle your desk so that people don't catch your eye as they walk past; at home, don't expect to find peace in the kitchen. Remove yourself from the household traffic pattern and settle in for some quiet time in a more remote area of the house.

■ *Anticipate the results of new occurrences.* If it's raining when you awaken one morning, get out the children's rain gear while you are getting out your own so that you don't need to stop and do it later. At work, if you are the right-hand person to someone who has been away, clear your schedule on the day of his or her return. That way you will have time available to help your boss catch up.

■ *To reduce receiving phone calls throughout the day, try letting people know when it is best to reach you.* At work, you may designate afternoons as a time when you are available for whatever comes your way, including all phone calls. At home, it may be convenient to make and receive phone calls from 7:30 to 8:30 P.M. When you speak to people—whether it is an aunt who lives across the country or your friend who checks in regularly—let them know that you are usually home then and that it is a good time for you to talk. You may be able to channel your phone calls into that time.

■ *Get your phone numbers listed in the Do Not Call Registry: www.donotcall.gov.*

■ *Trade off fielding calls with your spouse or a coworker.* The two of you can alternate answering the phone or dealing with other sorts of interruptions for an agreed-upon period of time.

managing the interruptions that occur

There will always be interruptions that you cannot prevent. What you can do, however, is manage them. Here are some strategies.

■ *Learn to keep your own priorities on top.* Try saying, "Could we talk about that in a few minutes? I have something here I need to finish." Or ask, "How much time do you need?" If the interrupter needs more than five minutes, ask that the two of you agree on a different time to meet.

■ *Learn to say, "Not now."* Often the interrupter hasn't even noticed that you are busy or that you are taking a well-deserved break. Say

time  booster

ENCOURAGE INDEPENDENCE

- Make family members and coworkers as independent of you as possible. Consider:

    What is the most frequent reason someone interrupts you?

    Is there a way to arrange for them to take care of the matter themselves?

- If coworkers come to you seeking information, is there a way they could find those answers on their own? Or could they e-mail you and you will get back to them when it is convenient? Or can the matter simply wait until you have finished your current task? If you are the employer or manager of a group of people, prepare a "what to know and where to find it" handbook answering the most commonly asked questions for a new employee.

- Establish systems that prevent the need for interruptions. If you have a coworker or an assistant with whom you work closely, establish a daily meeting time so that you can discuss what you are both working on during the day. Although there may still be some unexpected issues that come up that will require further discussion later in the day, you will have reduced the number of interruptions by covering much of the information at a scheduled meeting.

- In anticipation of children who may need a snack, try providing a child-size pitcher on a low shelf of the refrigerator to enable children four and up to pour milk or juice for themselves. Keep available cut-up fruit, peeled carrot sticks, and crackers just for the taking. Cups, bowls, and napkins can also be left where they are accessible to junior members of the family.

that you will help the person, and then estimate the time when you will be available. To seven-year-old Sarah who wants you to play a game, try saying, "I'll join you in thirty minutes." And then set a kitchen timer to help her keep track of how much longer it will be until you are able to join her. And to Matt at the office who needs some information about your travel schedule, try saying, "I'll give you those dates at lunchtime, after I am finished here."

- *Take charge.* Often interrupters could be helped rather quickly if they would just get to the point. Try asking, "How can I help you?" to help direct their thoughts and to establish that this is not a time for chatting.

- *Speak up.* If your boss is a frequent interrupter, dropping off more work for you to do, you will need to have priority discussions now and then. You might say, "I have been working on a plan for our sales conference and I know it is important, but with all the other things that have come up, I just haven't been able to finish what I need to. Could we talk about what I have left to do and what you need to have me finish first?" Like everyone else, bosses frequently focus on clearing their desks, not worrying about yours. Once the situation is brought to his or her attention, you may be pleasantly surprised by how reasonable your supervisor can be.

- *Analyze the interruption.* When you are interrupted, make the following evaluations:

  Am I the only one who can help this person?

  How much time will this take?

  If I let them interrupt me, what am I losing?

- *Don't prolong an interruption.* Once you know what is needed and have evaluated what you are going to do about it, go back to what you were doing. Often people succumb to the interruption and encourage the interrupter to stay. The next thing you know you are in the midst of a twenty-minute conversation about the person's trip to Alaska.

- *Consider what you can do once you are interrupted.* You can file while chatting with a coworker who has just returned from a trip. You can do a host of household tasks while the repairman is working. You can use your cell phone and return calls while doing chores almost anywhere in the house—from unloading the dishwasher to preparing a full meal to running upstairs to put pharmacy items away.

- *Involve the interrupter.* A coworker who ends up having to help you collate a report may think twice before dropping in unexpectedly, while a child or a spouse may actually be quite happy to be included in your project with a task geared to their level and interest.

- *Stand up.* If someone has dropped into your office "for just a minute," try standing up, which should discourage him or her from sitting down. If the interrupter has already taken a seat, then it should give the person the cue that it is time to leave. If that doesn't work, ask if he or she would like to walk somewhere with you. That limits the amount of your time the person can take because you are now in control of when you opt to turn around and walk back to your office.

- *Use teamwork.* If there is a well-known time-waster at your office, set up a system with colleagues. Ask that they phone you with an "emergency" five minutes or so after your talkative coworker has descended upon you.

protecting reasonable blocks of time

To have some interruption-free time, you first need to decide how much time you can reasonably protect, and then you need to safeguard it.

- At home and at work, screen calls through voice mail or an answering machine.

- Close the door. Consider buying or making a DO NOT DISTURB sign so that potential visitors will get the message.

- "Interrupt only if you are bleeding" is the rule in one family where the parents run a home-based business (and the children are old enough to recognize a real emergency).

- If you work in an open office without doors, go to an empty conference room or office for your interruption-free time or leave the premises. Some people go to the library or a coffee shop and get work done there.

sanity saver

MAINTAIN FOCUS DESPITE INTERRUPTIONS

Because interruptions are bound to happen, the challenge is to prevent a small interruption from becoming a major disruption. Here are a few ideas to help you better manage interruptions.

- If you are doing desk work or serious thinking when interrupted, quickly make a note of what your current thoughts were before looking up. If your work involves reading or reviewing material, mark where you left off.

- Get in the habit of breaking down tasks into smaller steps. If you know you stopped after step three, it will permit you to come back to the project more easily.

- If the interruption is something that must be taken care of, evaluate whether your response could be delayed for a bit while you finish what you are working on. If you must switch your focus to a new priority now, take a look at your calendar to reschedule time for the project you are abandoning.

- If you have been interrupted several times, it is very tempting to simply give up trying to work and quit. Unless you foresee that the day has simply gone out of control, try not to become discouraged. Go back and complete your goal for that day.

assessing your interruptions

If you are still puzzled about why your time is so fractured, conduct an interruption assessment. Keep a running log, noting the following:

Who interrupted you?

When?

Why?

How long were you disrupted?

After tracking your interruptions for a week, begin to look for patterns.

- Are the same people responsible for the majority of your interruptions? Once you recognize who is creating most of your interruptions, there are steps you can take to make them less dependent on you during specific blocks of time.

- Could their interruption have been anticipated? If you can anticipate their needs, you ought to be able to prevent the interruption.

- Could it have waited? Next time you will remember to say, "Not now, but later."

- If the disruption turns out to be something that affects you indirectly, see if there isn't some way to improve your situation. For example, if you work in an office that opens to a hallway where people gather to chat, try closing your door. If that isn't possible, ask nicely if they could move their conversation elsewhere for today. Over time, they will develop a new place to hang out.

overcoming the habit of self-interrupting

Self interrupting occurs when, in the process of trying to do one thing, you decide to focus on something else. Almost everyone can identify with the self-interrupting we do when on the Internet. How often have you been answering an e-mail, only to become curious about something . . . and the next thing you know, you've abandoned the e-mail you were trying to answer and clicked over to several other Web sites that attracted your attention, completely forgetting about your intention to answer the e-mail.

Unfortunately, this is only the most modern form of self-interrupting. We do it at work when we become distracted by a personal discussion when we've phoned someone for research; we do it at home when we come home with packages and go on to do something else before putting things away; we do it on our own time when we never finish our to-do list because we started watching something on television instead.

Self-interrupting generally becomes worse at two distinct times. The first instance occurs when you want to avoid something, because the interruption serves as an excellent form of procrastination. The second occurance is when you have been interrupted so often by forces beyond your control that you lose your ability to focus. As a result, you find that you are constantly interrupting yourself.

Making your environment more conducive to concentration will help you break the self-interrupting habit. Here's what you can do.

- If you are trying to complete desk work, make certain your desk surface is clear. If you remove temptation—that is, other things to do—from your sight, you will find it easier to stay on task.

- Before you start work, make certain you have the supplies or equipment you need. If you are packing up a box to be mailed and your labels are in one room and your tape is in another—offering an excellent opportunity for self-interrupting—the job will take extra time because you haven't collected what you need.

- Once you have established time to work on something, make a pact with yourself to focus on that project. If you have been in the habit of interrupting yourself a lot, set small goals. For example, you might say to yourself, "I'll work on this for fifteen minutes, and then I'll take a break" (or make a phone call or whatever you would rather be doing). By building up to longer work periods gradually, you will strengthen your power of concentration and your desire to focus time on what you need to do.

- Don't start another project without finishing the one you are working on.

- Concentration radiates its own protective shield. Coworkers or family members may walk in and realize that you are really busy. Don't look up, and resist the urge to begin a conversation by asking what they want. If they exhibit good sense by leaving you alone, let them.

- Even when you have been interrupted, try to get back to your work and meet whatever goal it is that you have set for the day.

- Don't procrastinate! (See the third thief.)

On days when our plans begin to unravel, we sometimes have trouble focusing on anything at all. The solution? Get involved in completing just one thing—maybe something as simple as opening the mail. After you experience the satisfaction of completing one task, you will find it easier to settle down and finish something else without constantly interrupting yourself and quitting before you have even begun.

the third thief of time: procrastination

There are many reasons why we procrastinate.

A task is overwhelming or too time-consuming.

We would rather be doing something else.

We lack the skills to do the task or we don't know how to get started.

We suffer from poor work habits.

So we wait, hoping that the task will change, be done by someone else, or simply go away. Perhaps Mark Twain said it best: "Never put off 'til tomorrow what you can do the day after tomorrow."

There are several basic steps you can take to help prevent procrastination.

- *Get organized.* This doesn't mean spending days straightening out your home or office; it means getting organized for a project you are about to undertake. For a new project, writing a list of the necessary steps or collecting all your documents in a file folder is often a good way to get organized. And remember, you don't need every detail to fall in place to get started.

- *Evaluate your work environment.* People often procrastinate because the environment is not conducive to getting things done. It is natural to hate filing if your drawers are so stuffed that you scrape your hand getting files in and out. And it is no wonder you are late paying your bills if you have to comb the house looking for what you did with them each month.

- *Break large tasks into small steps.* I often say that if you look at anything as a series of small steps, the task won't seem so overwhelming. Have you ever watched a child eat a piece of single-slice cheese by nibbling around the edges? That is what you need to do when starting large projects. Just remember that "a journey of a thousand miles begins with a single step."

- *Start the day with your most difficult task.* Once you complete that task, the rest of the day will be a breeze.

- *Make appointments with yourself.* Nothing gets done if you don't set aside time for it. If you have been intending to take up landscape painting and have procrastinated for years, it is because you never made an appointment with yourself to do it. Start now. Although fifteen- to forty-five-minute appointments are ideal for whatever you want to undertake, you can use as little as five minutes to assemble materials, to research a good art class, or to simply pick up the phone and make a few inquiries. Cell phones mean you can call people while waiting for a friend or while commuting, and otherwise make good use of time that might have been wasted.

- *Seize extra moments.* If by chance you find yourself with some extra time (an appointment is canceled or someone is late meeting you), take advantage of the unplanned-for moment by taking care of another step or two of a project.

- *Plan for leisure time and use it for leisure.* People sometimes procrastinate because they feel they "never get a break." By giving yourself some time off and relaxing, you will find you have less need to play hooky when you should be doing something else.

To further understand the tendency to procrastinate, it is helpful to have a better understanding of why you are doing it.

procrastination by accident

Lots of people don't intend to procrastinate—they just don't take action at a time when the task is still simple. People put off little things like responding to invitations, dealing with the last few pieces of mail, or putting away the craft items their toddler used for a project. They might be good time managers in other ways, but eventually these little projects mount up. Here are tips for avoiding accidental procrastination.

■ Because the items being put off are small tasks, do as many as you can when they come up. Invitations should be responded to immediately; filing a few papers can be done during a free moment; and the stack of mail should be completely taken care of every single day.

■ Use deadlines to your advantage. When a small item comes up, set an artificial deadline. You will find it much easier to accomplish.

■ Set aside twenty to thirty minutes daily for the so-called little stuff. By grouping miscellaneous phone calls or establishing a time when you can take care of small details, you will soon find that it is easy work to complete.

you're simply overwhelmed

Sometimes we just have so many things to do or our plate is so full we can't decide where to begin. At these times, we may look like workaholics, but we find we are working on the wrong task. I once heard this tendency described as "stomping on ants while starving the elephants."

You need to know how to get started on the right tasks.

■ *Make a list of the steps (or various aspects) of the job.* Next, break the project into more manageable steps. The job will become clearer and easier to handle.

■ *Jump right in.* When you are overwhelmed, the most difficult thing is to get started. If the project is new or immense, and you can't yet define any steps, start somewhere—anywhere. If you jump in, you will find that the assignment will become clearer to you.

■ *Don't expect to have a major block of time when you can "really get going with this."* Major blocks of time are very rare. Because you have broken the job into parts, it should be easier to find small chunks of time when you can do one or two things, working toward your major goal. Even five minutes can be enough to accomplish one step.

■ *Ask for clarification or better instructions.* People often procrastinate because some aspect of a job is unclear. The sooner you understand what you are to do, the easier the work will be.

- *Ask whether there is a simpler way to perform the tasks.* Sometimes procrastinators take a roundabout route when there is a straight path.

- *At the end of one work session, make a note of what you will do next.* If you plan your tasks for the next session, you will find that your desire to procrastinate subsides.

when you just don't want to do it

From calling for a dental appointment to diving into a volunteer project, there are many times when procrastinators delay because they are hoping that the task will go away or will be done by someone else. Of course, this rarely happens. We end up simply putting off what we don't want to do—but dreading the fact that we will, at some point, have to do it. The dentist is booked up, so you must take an appointment that isn't very convenient. The volunteer project still has to be completed, but it's left with lots of loose ends because of the lack of time.

Here is how to complete a task when you just don't want to do it.

- Ask yourself: "What could happen if I don't do this?" If the consequences are negative—imagine having a cavity worsen or disappointing someone who is depending on you—the poor outcome should spur you to action. On the other hand, maybe not doing the task isn't so terrible. There are always some to-do items in your master notebook that have become less important. Yes, you were really angry that the town snowplow dumped a huge mound of snow at the bottom of your freshly shoveled driveway, but are you still convinced a letter of complaint is worth your time? (The best way to judge the importance of a task is to review what you are likely to gain from it.) Cross off all low-level priorities that you have put off.

- If you decide you must do it, is there someone to whom you could delegate the task? If not, take action on your own as soon as possible. You will be amazed at how great you will feel after putting it behind you!

- Find a way to make the task more pleasurable. Some people return telephone calls or listen to music or an audiobook while doing a boring household task such as ironing or polishing silver.

■ Some types of unpleasant tasks can be accomplished during time you might waste anyway. One mother carries the day's mail with her, along with a letter opener and a pen for making notes. "I go through all our mail while my children are in dance class or karate. That way I never have to set aside time to do it at home."

■ Recurring tasks that you don't enjoy such bill paying or filling out expense reports for work should be written on your calendar so that you have a certain day devoted to taking care of it. Tackling these chores will become easier if you have established a routine. If you aren't already doing so, explore paying your bills online (see chapter 11). Once you have the system set up, it will definitely save you time.

■ Build in rewards for yourself. If you are truly phobic about going to the dentist, promise yourself some small gift for making the appointment; establish a larger one for the evening after you have been to the appointment.

"i work best under pressure"

Some people claim they work best under pressure—they like the adrenaline rush when a project must be completed by the next day. Yet things seldom work out the way they expect. I often hear about the negative outcomes from my clients.

"I thought I could finish it in time, but I got a really bad cold three days before it was due, and there was no way I could work while I was sick."

"When we go on vacation, I always pack at about two in the morning. By the time I get on the plane, I am anxious and exhausted, and by the time the plane is taking off, I realize I've forgotten something."

"I was so busy I couldn't shop before Christmas Eve, and by that time they had sold out of what my daughter really wanted."

If you are a Last-Minute Louie, you know it. To reform, you must resolve to live a different way. The client who wasn't able to surprise her daughter with that one dreamed-of holiday present was highly motivated to change, as was the fellow who got sick right before his project's due date. Maybe you haven't had a bad experience yet, but you know what those night-before jitters are like, worrying about whether you will finish or will your work be good enough? Here are some additional suggestions.

- *Write down how working under pressure makes you feel.* Does it keep you awake? Do you get an upset stomach? Are you tired afterward? Are you grumpy with your spouse or the kids? Or do you worry because you really didn't have enough time to do a good job? This exercise should serve as a reminder as to why a change of habit is advised.

- *Break up your task into steps with interim deadlines.* Then, set your final deadline a day or two earlier than necessary. Plan something fun for the day or night before the real due date. Now instead of sweating out whether you will be finished, you can look forward to lunch with a friend or a movie because you know you will be finished.

- *Ask your spouse or a colleague to help you by taking note of your due dates and making you accountable to them.* (After you've changed your habits, this step won't be necessary, but it's a great way to bring about reform.)

Once you experience the pleasure of being able to relax the night before you teach a special seminar, leave on a trip, or celebrate the holidays, you will never go back to your former lifestyle.

procrastinating by habit

Some people simply procrastinate from habit. Studies show that 20 percent of American adults suffer from this malady—they simply put off things that need to be done. It's the most difficult kind of procrastination because the habits have become second nature. These people have poor work habits and are easily distracted because they've never learned to settle down and focus on a task.

If you have fallen into the trap of habitually procrastinating, here is how to strengthen your self-discipline and sharpen your concentration skills.

- To change a habit, you must start with something manageable. Select a relatively pleasant small task on which you have been procrastinating. Establish the number of minutes you think it will take and promise yourself to do absolutely nothing else with the time until you have finished the task. Don't take or make a phone call; don't touch an extraneous piece of paper. Do only the task at hand.

■ If you have been procrastinating on something like exercising or cleaning out a closet, chances are that you've been berating yourself for never getting around to these tasks. Make a bargain with yourself: you will work on it for no less than five minutes and no more than fifteen minutes on the first day. (Remember to break a task like closet cleaning down into small parts: straighten a shelf, sort through the twenty belts you have on a hook, and so forth.) This brief exposure will show you that performing the activity wasn't so terrible and that you made some progress. As soon as you take some positive action, your anxiety will disappear. Going back to it the next day will be less stressful.

■ Refer to chapters 7 and 16 regarding a tidy environment. People who procrastinate habitually frequently work in a cluttered environment where other incomplete tasks attract attention and take time when they shouldn't.

■ If the telephone is your primary distraction, use a family member, a colleague, or voice mail to screen calls. If that doesn't help, work on your task in a quiet environment and turn off your cell phone. The public library will insist on this practice, but you can follow it elsewhere—for example, going to a conference room at work or the park in nice weather will do you no good if you make yourself available by cell phone or e-mail.

Over time you will find that you are less easily distracted and more capable of concentrating on the task. If you find your poor habits creeping back, consider whether you are particularly tired or stressed. For reminders on how to get back on track, reread this section of the chapter or the next section, Helpful Tips for Procrastinators.

helpful tips for procrastinators

Sometimes it's hard to come up with a way to get going; because you've procrastinated for so long, it seems as if you'll never get started. Here are some ways to jump-start your effort.

■ *Jump right in.* Pick any step that appeals to you.

- *Set a time to begin the project.* It is important to just get started.

- *Start small.* Work on only a part of the task in small units of time.

- *Build the task into your daily rhythm.* Fifteen to twenty minutes every day will make it a consistent part of your schedule and help keep you going. For example, if you exercise every morning before breakfast, you will soon reach a point where you won't even think about not exercising.

- *Use a kitchen timer.* Tell yourself, "I can do anything for twenty minutes." Set the timer and get started. When the bell rings, stop. Chances are that you will have gotten enough done that you will have a good idea of what you want to do with your twenty minutes tomorrow. Should you keep working past the twenty minutes? If you can actually finish the task with another twenty minutes invested, then it would be wise to devote the extra time. Otherwise, it's better to accomplish it in regularly scheduled intervals rather than burn yourself out early on.

- *Inspire yourself.* Develop a positive attitude and keep focused on the benefits of getting the task accomplished.

- *Shock yourself.* Ask yourself, "What are the consequences if I don't get started?" The answer may jolt you into action.

- *Use a buddy system.* Ask a friend or a colleague to nudge you into action and to check on your progress.

- *Ask for help.* Work with someone else or create a team. The work will go more quickly and be more fun.

- *Promise yourself a reward for getting started.*

part

two

make time around the house

household storage to holiday

planning in half the time

6

household storage

*f*uturists tell us that one day soon our houses will run themselves and save us time in the process. Already we have thermostats that operate on their own time clock, preheating a room in the morning for our wake-up and cooling it down at night when everyone is asleep. We have coffeemakers that can be set to perk at the time we get up in the morning, and we have slow cookers that we can set at breakfast so that dinner will be ready when we come home at night. Robotic vacuums actually work pretty well for cleaning the floors, and do-it-itself robot lawn mowers are on the way.

But leaping forward, things are going to get even better. Inventors are working on a refrigerator that will not only tell us that we are low on milk but will place a grocery order without our having to pick up the phone. And some types of prepared foods will come with electronic tags to inform the microwave how to cook the dish—no thinking necessary on the part of the "cook." As for lawn watering, you'll soon go to your computer to program the schedule, and if you're out of town and hear it has been raining back home, no problem—just hop on your laptop (with wireless access) to turn off your home system from wherever you are.

Home automation certainly offers great promise for the future—and great headaches when it malfunctions—but in the meantime I will tell you that the stories my clients share with me when I visit their homes are always the same.

People are overwhelmed by their stuff. They waste a lot of time worrying about it, moving it around, and looking for what they can't find. Although a few clients have tidy kitchens or impeccably neat living rooms, not long after my arrival they all lead me to the parts of the home that are driving them batty. Closets, family rooms, home offices, and the garage are prime areas that are difficult to manage. More often then not, the households I visit are drowning in clutter.

The point of neat-as-a-pin households is not just to have a neat-as-a-pin household. The point is to be able to find what you want when you want it and to be able to live comfortably. Imagine the pleasure of coming home from a bookstore or the drugstore and having more than enough space to put away your purchases.

I always tell my clients, the more items you can easily store, the more usable and comfortable your house. You'll soon find that when your home is well organized, you'll be eager to return things to their proper place.

Here are a few general storage guidelines to keep in mind.

■ There are two rules of placement.

1. *Stash it near where you use it.* Try to set up each room so that within a few steps you have access to anything you need. Place mats should be kept in a drawer near the dining table; pad, pencil, and the telephone book near the telephone; umbrellas and boots near the front door, the back door, or in the mud room (whichever you use regularly); spare sheets in a linen closet near the bedrooms; extra towels in a closet in or near the bathroom; and so on.

2. *Employ the "how-often-do-you-use-it" rule to decide how and where to put things away.* Items used daily should be most accessible—for example, on the shelves that are at eye level. Items used weekly, like cleaning supplies and bed linens, can be stored at squatting and tiptoe levels. Rarely used items like

holiday decorations or a punch bowl can be stored very high in closets or in more remote parts of the house such as the basement, the attic, or the garage.

- For less frequently used items, rent or borrow, don't own. From folding tables to garden tillers, most items used occasionally can be rented, saving storage space, maintenance, and money.

- Every household has items coming in (new purchases, incoming packages) and items going out (dry cleaning, library books to return, shoes in need of repair). These become clutter if you don't assign a place where you can put them. A table, a cabinet, a shelf, or a chair near the door you use most frequently is ideal. Dedicate a tote bag for errand use, and start filling it as you think of the tasks that need to be accomplished.

- Teach family members to lay out everything they need for the next day so that no one is doing a last-minute, time-eating hunt for a schoolbook or homework papers.

family room neatness

Every home needs a room that is comfy and lived in, but there is a fine line between "lived in" and "messy."

- Consider how you use the room and plan for the items that are used there. A coffee table with a shelf beneath can provide an easy spot to slip the newspaper or any magazines that are read in the room. Built-in shelving or drawers can provide storage for books, games, CDs, DVDs, and other amusements.

- Toy baskets are great for baby and toddler toys that are often too bulky to put in a drawer or on a shelf.

- Do a "clutter sweep" through the room at least twice a week. Ask everyone to put away items that have been left out.

- If you permit snacks or eating in the family room, all family members should cooperate in a "getting the dishes back to the kitchen promptly" rule.

sanity saver

THE UNIVERSAL REMOTE

If you're like most people, you've added to your household electronics collection one item at a time—first the TV, then the VCR or TiVo system, then a CD player and a DVD player, and so on. At this point, you probably have three or four remote controls to keep track of. There is a solution. Switch to a universal remote control that will operate all the equipment. These remotes are well designed and easy to use, and you will no longer need to keep track of several different remote controls.

Dedicate a small container to hold the remote control, the television schedule, and a marker or pen (to highlight the shows you plan to watch) within easy reach.

great storage ideas

Having a space and a place for all your household items will help you maintain a neat and orderly house. One of the best ways to do this is to use adequate storage containers to neatly manage all your stuff. You can find handy and innovative containers and storage systems for every room of your house at your local office supply store, department store, or even online.

- Inexpensive rolling carts are handy in every room for making stored items mobile, visible, and accessible.

- Use a wide variety of boxes, bags, containers, crates, cubbies, hooks, and lots of shelving to accommodate what you need.

- Keep a box handy to temporarily store items to be given away or donated. You'll find that you're better at weeding out unwanted items if you have a specific place to put them.

- Store gift wrap and supplies in a large, shallow container under the bed or in a basket-style caddy that can be easily carried to a work space when needed.

organizing your rooms and your belongings

Following are the areas in many homes that get cluttered and messy easily and the steps you can take to make sure that these spaces stay organized.

the bathroom

- Where space allows, install shelving and cabinets to store as many items as possible.

- Keep the bathroom counter as clutter-free as possible.

- Use caddies or small baskets to group and hold items such as makeup, hair-care supplies, cleaning products, and so on.

- Keep items used in the shower and bath in a shower caddy.

- Mesh bags are ideal for holding bath toys. Buy the kind with a drawstring so you can hang it over the faucet when not using the toys.

- Extra rolls of toilet paper should be within easy reach of the toilet in a cabinet or kept in a basket sitting on the back of the toilet or hanging on the wall. Keep spare boxes of tissues in a linen closet or under the sink.

- Store overflow items from the bathroom in a see-through plastic shoe bag or plastic bin in the linen closet.

- Some families find it easier to use a different color towel for each child.

medicines and first aid

If you have children in the household, "childproof" has to trump "convenience" when it comes to putting away medicines and first-aid supplies.

- Select a storage spot that is inaccessible to your child as well as to any children who might be visiting. This may be a high shelf in the parents' bedroom or in a cabinet or a closet that is secured with a childproof lock.

- Although a bathroom medicine chest is the classic place for keeping medicines, it is actually not ideal. Not only are medicine chests hard to secure so that children can't get into them, but the steam and humidity that are created by bathing or showering can negatively affect the composition of some medicines. It's better to choose a dry spot elsewhere in the house.

- Once a year—for example, just before the winter cold and flu season—sort through the medications and check expiration dates. Note what needs to be replaced.

- Arrange medicines by remedy. Group together pain relievers, cold remedies, and cough drops in separate spots so that a quick check of the area will show you what you have and what you may need.

- A tackle box can be a great place for first-aid equipment. You can put fabric elastic bandages and/or gauze rolls in the bigger section below, with ointments, scissors, and adhesive bandages up above.

the hall closet

- Group seasonal coats by length to allow for some accessible floor storage and so that you can double hang in parts of the closet.

- Hang children's coats and accessories on the closet door at their height.

- Place children's accessories in see-through shoe bags on the back of the door or in baskets or bins on the closet floor.

- Store adult accessories such as gloves, scarves, and purses in baskets or bins on the closet shelf.

- Keep boots in containers so that they will stay in place.

- Use hooks, pegs, or a rack inside the closet or on the back of the door to store umbrellas, a flashlight, a lint brush, and scarves.

the linen closet

- Purchase sheets for each bed or bed size in a different color so that you can quickly connect the right bed and sheet set by sight. That way you'll never again find yourself putting twin sheets on a double bed.

- Fold sheets in sets with the pillowcases tucked inside the two sheets.

HOSTING GUESTS

Create a guest box. Since few people have guest rooms but many people have guests, make it easier to welcome guests by dedicating an under-bed storage box to keep extra linens, towels, blankets, and even niceties such as soap and shampoo for those times when someone extra is spending the night.

- Stack towels by size and color, and group by person or room. Place infrequently used towels (beach and guest towels) on a less accessible shelf.
- Remove worn towels and sheets from active storage and put them to use for bathing the pet or washing the car or to use as rags.
- Use stackable clear containers to house smaller items arranged by category.
- Use the back of the door for storing the iron and ironing board.
- Store bulky items such as a vacuum, stool, or hamper on the closet floor.

the clothes closet

I've seen more closets in my lifetime than you can imagine, so I can say with great certainty: it's better to have a few terrific outfits you feel good in than to bother trying to manage a closet bursting with excess.

Clear Out

- If you haven't worn something in over a year, you'll probably never wear it again. Donate or discard those items.
- Put out-of-season clothing on high shelves or store in a spare closet.
- After organizing, assess what you need: More lighting? A stool? Hooks? Pegs? More shelves? Shoe racks?

Put Away with Care

- Double hang clothes if space allows.
- Face all hangers in the same direction to avoid tangling.

- Arrange clothing by category, color, and length. Hang dark to light and separate solids from prints.

- To save time, keep outfits together—for example, blouse with suit, and so forth. Some men get help matching up ties and specific suits and then hang them next to each other so they won't make the wrong decision in the morning.

- If you have a big shoe collection, it can be difficult to find the shoes you want when you need them. Buy stackable clear shoebox-size storage boxes to store your shoes. Another option is to photograph your shoes and tape the picture of the style on the outside of the box.

- Store scarves on hangers to save space and to prevent wrinkles.

- Hatboxes work well to store bathing suits, belts, dressy handbags and extra items for your purse such as hankies, and spare eyeglass cases. Label the box on the top and on the side so you'll know what it contains.

- During the warm months, store bulky items such as sweaters in under-bed containers.

Maintain What You Start

- When you undress, set aside clothing that needs to be cleaned, mended, or ironed, and shoes that need to be polished.

- Sort out at the end of each season. Be tough about what needs to be discarded. In late March, you'll still remember that those long-sleeved shirts were looking dingy. By October, you may be less critical. Give away gently used items, turn the frayed ones into cleaning cloths, and start a list of new pieces you'll need for next fall/winter. Do the same thing for the spring/summer season.

jewelry

I visit many houses where my client eventually shows me a drawer or a jewelry box that is just heaping with stuff: earrings that may or may not have mates, necklaces that are tangled, bracelets that are tarnished. And as we talk, the client will point out items from high school—and I always wonder if she really thinks she will wear that 1970s-style ring again?

Most of us don't have the type of jewelry that is so valuable that it should be saved forever. Jewelry is just like any other fashion accessory: fine if you love it and feel good in it but dispensable if you find you no longer wear it very often. If you paid a significant sum for it, sell it to a secondhand dealer. If not, donate it with other clothing items.

Here's how to get—and keep—your jewelry box in order.

- As you sort through your jewelry, chances are you'll find pieces you never remembered you had. Clear out what you'll never again use. Toss items in bad condition or earrings with missing mates. (If the pieces are valuable, real silver or gold and gemstones can be sold by weight or size.) After you have finished disposing of your discards, pull out what you wear most often so that you can put it in an accessible storage location.

- To make your jewelry easy to find, it should be stored in a container that has small sections. The traditional choice is a real jewelry box. However, you can also use a tackle box from a hardware store or the little drawer systems that hold nuts and bolts. That way you'll be able to see and find what you want to wear.

- There are many jewelry stands available for hanging items so that they are accessible and convenient. You can also hang necklaces on hooks on the wall so you can see what you have. It provides "art" for the wall space and convenience for you. Remember that jewelry you can see is jewelry you will wear.

the night table

One of my clients called and confessed he needed me after being startled out of a deep sleep when a stack of books on his bedside table finally toppled on him. I doubt he is the only person out there guilty of excessive nightstand clutter.

sanity saver

HOUSEHOLD MANAGEMENT

There are two ways to stay on top of household management if you do them regularly:

1. Put things away.
2. Weed out constantly!

■ Take a good look at what you're storing by your bedside. Toss, donate, or store elsewhere the year-old magazines and the books you've never gotten around to reading.

■ In and on the bedside unit, keep only the necessities such as tissues, lip balm, flashlight, reading material, notepaper and pen, eyeglasses, and alarm clock.

books

If your house is overflowing with books or you just don't have enough space to store the books you do have, you need to create a better system.

■ To save time, presort your books so that you don't have to organize those you don't want to keep. Walk past all your current book storage spaces and pull from the shelves the books that you know you'll never read (or read again). Chances are this task will automatically clear some space for you. Donate the unwanted books to schools, hospitals, libraries, and so forth.

■ Measure the amount of available "shelf feet" in your home. Then, calculate the number of needed "book feet"—that is, how many feet would be required to store your current books—so you can plan accordingly.

■ Look for little-used space in your home to add in bookshelves.

■ Invest in heavy bookends. Then you can display or store books on a table or the back of a desk, not just in bookcases.

■ Decide on categories—separate fiction titles from nonfiction, and break nonfiction into sensible units like "travel," "art history," and so on. You can put art history in the spare bedroom and the gardening books in the family room, for example.

■ Don't pack shelves tightly, otherwise your books will become too difficult to retrieve. Also, a little breathing room permits you to add new books without rearranging the old ones.

■ Don't be tempted to shelve with a front and a back line of books—you'll never find what is hidden behind.

■ Many people designate a reading shelf where they put the books they want to consider reading next. That way you get a bookstore-like pleasure when you survey the tempting possibilities, but you haven't endangered yourself by sleeping next to a towering pile.

7

clearing the clutter

Whether my clients live in small apartments or palatial homes, I find that they all—male or female, mature or just starting out—have one complaint in common: they are tired of dealing with all their clutter. Unfortunately, clutter is a major side effect of modern life. People often complain to me that they don't have enough storage space, but storage is only a small part of the problem. We all have too much paper and paraphernalia coming into our homes, and figuring out where to put this stuff causes stress.

One of the most shocking apartments I've encountered recently was the combined home of two people in their thirties who had just married. She was moving into his space, and I cannot begin to describe how much stuff they intended to pack into this one-bedroom apartment— from golf clubs and a double supply of luggage to dishes for far more than two. They hired me to help them plan out their space, but they were so busy putting things up for auction on eBay that it was hard for them to concentrate on much else.

Another nightmare I encountered was an apartment in Florida where stacks of books and papers lined every wall in the house. To get to one room, I was led through a passageway between stacks of stuff. It was a lovely apartment with two bathrooms, but they used only one. Why? Because the guest bathroom shower stall was filled with papers, and the resident was embarrassed for people to go in there and see how bad her situation had become.

The problem is that the more stuff you have, the longer it takes you to clean around it and find a place to store all of it. Whether it's the clothing in the back of your closet that you haven't worn in three years or the unread mail that is building up on the kitchen counter or the sports equipment you no longer use or the bridal shower favor you didn't want and have no idea what to do with—all these extra possessions contribute to a cluttered mind-set. The more you are able to pare down your possessions to the things you love and actually have space for, the more time you will create for yourself.

Decluttering is also enormously liberating!

This chapter begins with an emergency plan for the arrival of company. It continues with a more long-term solution to fighting clutter.

short-order pickup

Yikes! Company is coming! Here's a fifteen-minute plan for making your home presentable quickly when friends or family are stopping by.

- Take a big bag or basket and simply walk around your home picking up items as quickly as possible. Later that evening or by the weekend, be sure to sort and put everything away.

- Take a spray cleaner and paper towels and stop into both the bathroom and the kitchen. A spritz and a polish in these two rooms will make a big difference.

- Focus on tidying, not cleaning. Even your mother-in-law probably won't notice a little extra dust, but she will notice if magazines are everywhere and stacks of mail are sitting unopened.

- Plump up the couch pillows and throw pillows and fold any afghans you use for snuggling.

- Change hand towels in the bathroom, wipe the sink and the counter, and refill the soap dispenser.

- Put dirty dishes in the dishwasher.

- Focus on items at eye level when cleaning—that's what people notice.

- Spray-clean tabletops and run the vacuum quickly, but only if necessary.

how to declutter simply and easily

To begin to weed out clutter without having to devote hours to this project, write down the top four areas—keeping the areas you mention small, such as "kitchen counter," "junk drawer," or "closet floor"—of your household where clutter builds up. On your to-do list for each week of the upcoming month, write down one of these listed areas to tackle. Because the areas you've listed are relatively small, you should be able to weed through them in fifteen to sixty minutes.

As you sort, keep asking yourself: Do I love it? Do I need it? Is it something I'll use or wear? Do I have a place for it? One client who really embraced the cleaning-out process suggests going through your possessions as if it were moving day. She asks herself, "Would I want to bother with wrapping or packing it for a move?" If not, it gets tossed, recycled, or donated. Here are some other examples of how to declutter your space.

In your closet. If you haven't worn something in a year, donate it. If you just can't part with it, move it to a storage closet and wait a few months. Chances are it will be easier to part with then.

Living room or bedroom bric-a-brac. The Elvis snow globe a friend brought you from Memphis was good for a laugh, but after a couple of months, give it a toss.

Birthday cards. Display for a week then out they go. (Store the ones with the personal notes in a keepsake box if you can't bear to part with them.)

Kitchen junk drawer. It's okay to have a miscellaneous drawer, but try to weed out the true junk.

Magazines. Make it a rule that when the new issue arrives, the old one gets donated. Keep current issues in a conveniently located magazine rack.

As you declutter your home, you will face the dilemma of whether to keep, toss, or donate. Sometimes my clients get totally bogged down with having to make decisions. Keep in mind that much of what you sort through can probably go in the trash. If you find some decent things, set them aside in a donation pile. Here is a warning: If you have second thoughts and decide to hold on to something because you might need or want it one day, chances are good it can be tossed. When in doubt, toss it out.

If you're having trouble deciding, put the items in a box that you can store in the basement or garage. Date the box to "Keep until _____." By that time, it will be clear whether the item is a keepsake that deserves storage space or whether it's time for it to be tossed or given away. Another option is to photograph items you've enjoyed but don't want to store anymore. The photo can provide the memories of the item, but you don't have to worry about storing it anymore.

The Internet can help in your efforts to declutter your home. Try selling what you can on eBay. Remember that one man's trash is another

time booster

SHORT-ORDER ROOM PICKUP

Here are some additional strategies for decluttering a room in a reasonable amount of time.

- Use the "clock" technique. Stand at the entrance of the room and designate a spot as twelve o'clock. Then start working your way around the face of the clock.

- Designate a temporary "junk chair." Choose one spot (perhaps a chair) and start piling up everything that doesn't belong in that room. Then start systematically sorting and putting away.

- Clean up according to destination. Go around the room with a basket, loading up on items based on where they should be put away—all kitchen items in the first round, all children's room items on the next round, and so forth.

man's treasure. You might as well profit from the excess. You can also post unwanted items on the Freecycle Network (www.freecycle.org). Posting is free. You must be willing to give the items away for free, but whoever takes the item is responsible for getting it off your property. This can be a time and energy saver with bigger items like that gigantic sofa bed you no longer have room for. Using this site also helps to reduce the number of unwanted items filling our landfills.

As you begin to declutter small sections of your household, you'll find that it will be faster and easier to keep those areas clean. Most people also feel inspired by the process. At the end of the first month, you can make a new list of four areas to declutter—and if one area is filling with clutter again, simply put it back on your list to clean out again.

enlist an anticlutter partner

Some people realize that five minutes into a project, they will lose interest. If that's you, you can hire a professional organizer—see the Web site for the National Association of Professional Organizers (www.napo.net) to locate professionals in your area—or you can team up with a friend. You go to your friend's house one Saturday afternoon, and then your friend comes to your house the following week.

- Set a time limit for how long you'll work, and select the area to attack. (You can move on to another area if there is time.)

- Whether you are tackling a closet, the kitchen counters, or bookshelves, work systematically.

- The person functioning as the coach needs to provide moral support and encouragement for items that are rarely used. (Have a box for the can't-quite-part-with-it items. That way the owner can put the box in the garage for six months and reevaluate those items later on.) The coach can help with the cleaning and organizing, since the owner of the clutter will be busy with decision making.

- Plan to go out for coffee or take a walk at the end of the session so that the two of you have something to look forward to as the work progresses.

keep clutter under control

Here are some steps to help keep clutter from controlling your life.

- Follow a "one in, one out" rule. If you buy a new coat, it's time to get rid of the old one. Keeping an old one around "just in case" only adds to your overall clutter.

- Keep a donations shopping bag in your closet for items you want to donate. Whenever you pull out something you don't really like or don't want anymore, add it to the shopping bag. When the bag is full, you can drop it off at a local donation center.

- Incoming mail is a huge part of everyone's clutter. See chapter 11 for more information.

- Establish baskets (small, medium, and large) in a central location, such as near the stairs if you live in multistory home. Use the baskets to hold items that accumulate during the week. Then be sure to empty the baskets and put away the contents each weekend.

- Weekends are hard on households. There is nothing worse than waking up Monday morning and realizing that the week is starting and the house is a mess. Here's what to do. Make an appointment with your spouse and/or family to pick up the household late Sunday afternoon or early evening. That way you can start fresh for the week. With young family members, try the Cleanup Game. Late Sunday afternoon, send the kids off to check around the house and identify the areas that need to be picked up or the chores that need to be done. Write each item on a piece of paper such as "fold laundry" or "pick up games in family room." Once the tasks have been identified and written down, each family member gets his or her assignment by drawing one of the slips of paper from a bowl or a hat. Then announce that all chores must be finished before dinner.

- Try living with a new rule: Leave each room a little neater than you found it. After you have dinner, make certain the kitchen is orderly and ready for the next day. If you've been watching television in the family room, tidy the magazines you were looking at and fluff the pillows on your way out.

8

housework quick and easy

Although no newspaper article ever mentioned, "And she— or he—kept a perfect house," I've been in enough homes to know that we all need to keep up with the housework. A home that is overrun with dust and cobwebs and has dirty dishes in the sink is simply not welcoming. And a home filled with clutter wastes time when you've lost something—a library book? a glove? the phone bill? your jury notice?—amid the stacks of stuff piled anywhere and everywhere. (If clutter is your issue, read chapter 7.)

And, of course, this type of environment is not conducive to cleaning— the picked-up house is the house that can be kept clean with a minimum of bother. The goal of this chapter is to show you how to streamline the cleaning process so that you can enjoy the benefits of a pleasant home environment without spending a lot of time on it.

your daily routine

The best gift you can give yourself is a simple daily routine that takes little time but provides the benefit of keeping things relatively clean.

- *Make your bed when you get up.* If you pull up the sheet and blanket as you get out of bed and shake out the bedspread or the comforter, you now have one less chore to do as you get ready for the day.

- *Keep a cleaning cloth or a roll of paper towels under the sink in the bathroom.* It takes thirty seconds after washing in the morning to wipe down the sink, the faucets, and the counter. The bathroom will need serious scrubbing less frequently if you clean and polish as you go.

- *Clean up spills when they happen in the kitchen.* The spilled item that may slow you down for a couple minutes in the morning will take ten to fifteen minutes to clean up if it has time to dry and harden.

- *Keep out the dirt in the first place.* Have a "no shoes on in the house" rule, and sweep the garage area once a week. When you vacuum, go over the doormats both inside and out. If the dirt doesn't come in, you don't have to spend time getting it out.

- *Toward the end of the day, take just five to ten minutes to straighten up around the house.* Take out that day's newspapers. Over the course of the week, you'll find you have less picking up to do overall, and this small daily investment of time will reap noticeable rewards. Children also need to be taught to pick up and put away each day. (More about this practice in chapter 20.)

tips to find time to clean

Although we all might long for a maid, most of us have to clean our houses ourselves—or with help from family members. Here are ways to schedule in cleaning time without having it consuming your life.

- *Put housework on your schedule.* While some people use Saturday mornings for errands and cleaning-type chores, other people prefer to free up Saturday mornings by fitting chores in at other times during the week such as early mornings or evenings. Spell out what tasks need to be done weekly, and write down those chores or times when completing them is convenient for you.

- *Don't clean what you don't like.* Do a room-by-room evaluation and toss items you no longer consider of interest—the cactus plant from your old job, the carved figure from two boyfriends ago, and the artificial flowers can all be tossed. (Also see chapter 7 for advice on clearing out the clutter.)

■ *Time yourself to see how long it takes to do certain chores.* This will give you an idea of how long you need to allow for particular tasks. If you know it takes you about fifteen minutes to empty wastebaskets and wipe down the bathrooms, you'll be able to fit that in when you have a few odd minutes before dinner, for example.

■ *Divide big tasks into smaller jobs.* For example, cleaning out the whole refrigerator is a medium-size job. Rather than thinking of when you can clean the whole thing, break the job into parts: wipe down all the shelves one evening; the next evening, empty out the shelves on the door and clean them. On the third evening, you can address the freezer.

■ *Invest in a small vacuum cleaner that you can take out quickly for spot cleaning.* If you can take care of a task quickly, you'll find it much easier to do.

■ *Work as part of a team.* (See the section on chores on page 99.)

■ *Multitask while talking on the phone.* You can clean out a drawer or a file, sew on a button, fold laundry, cut up vegetables, or pack a bag lunch. Any simple chore that needs doing can be accomplished quickly and more pleasantly if you're entertained.

■ *Consider it a twofer.* Housework really is good exercise. If you're doing a major vacuuming, cleaning out the garage, or dusting high

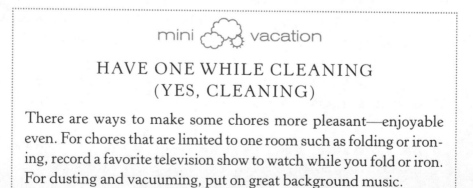

mini vacation

HAVE ONE WHILE CLEANING
(YES, CLEANING)

There are ways to make some chores more pleasant—enjoyable even. For chores that are limited to one room such as folding or ironing, record a favorite television show to watch while you fold or iron. For dusting and vacuuming, put on great background music.

and low, you can skip the gym that day as you will have already gotten your exercise.

■ *Entertain.* If you plan a party, you will have a lot of motivation to get the house in order for it—and you'll have a good time! (Start your cleaning and pickup process a couple days ahead so that you won't be exhausted on the night of the party.)

■ *Clean in moderation.* While homes need a really good cleaning now and then (to reduce allergies and fight mold), there are no rules that say you have to wipe baseboards once a week or dust all the books on the bookshelves. Clean the house well enough, and then consider hiring a service to come in to deep clean once or twice a year.

quick-cleaning methods

When it comes to cleaning their homes, most people want to finish the job as quickly as possible to have time for more enjoyable pursuits. With a little bit of planning and organization, you can reduce the time spent on household chores. These tips can show you how.

■ *Make cleaning convenient.* Gather your supplies in a caddy so that you have rags, a multipurpose cleaning spray, gloves, sponges, and any other tools you need. Invest in a good vacuum so you can work as efficiently as possible. Consider adding a thirty-foot extension cord to the vacuum so that you can roll farther than one room with it. You might also find that an apron with pockets can come in handy. The pockets can hold the little items you find as you go around the house.

■ *Learn to work in an organized fashion.* Professionals always work clockwise, from top to bottom.

■ *Collect the trash from all over the house.*

■ *Clean bathrooms first.* A clean bathroom really shows the shine, which will motivate you to do more. Be sure to change the towels.

■ *Think small.* Deal with small jobs before they turn into big ones. The best example is keeping things picked up. If you put things away every single day (or go through the mail every single day), you won't ever have to face a huge buildup. And of course, keeping things tidy will reduce your cleaning time because you don't have to pick up first.

- *Don't waste time scrubbing* pans. Soak pans with burned-on food in baking soda and a small amount of water and they will become easier to clean.

- *Double up.* Wipe the tub ring while you're waiting for the tub to drain. Clean the sink while you're waiting for water to boil.

- *Dampen your dustpan before you sweep debris into it.* This trick keeps the dust from drifting back out.

- *If you're pressed for time, commit to fifteen to thirty minutes.* You'll be amazed at what you can get done in that time.

    Dust the furniture.

    Vacuum.

    Give the kitchen a good once-over—counters, table, and floor.

    Iron most of what you would need for the week. (Careful folding as clothing comes out of the dryer results in less time devoted to ironing.)

    Change the sheets on the beds.

bathroom cleaning secrets

Second only to the kitchen (to which I've devoted a whole chapter), the bathroom is a heavily trafficked room that can either look great or absolutely terrible, with water spattered on the mirror, soap scum in the tub, and mounds of towels on the floor. Here's how to keep your bathroom shining.

- Use furniture or car wax on shower doors and ceramic wall tiles. The wax will reduce the problems of soap scum, lime, and mineral deposits. These areas will stay clean longer.

- Cut a thin sponge to fit inside the soap dishes in the sink, shower, and tub; the sponge will catch the scummy, soapy runoff. Instead of scrubbing these hard-to-clean areas, just rinse the soap scum out of the sponges.

- Purchase a spray cleaner and a mold fighter for each bathroom to make it more convenient to clean up regularly.

- Invest in a good quality squeegee to use on shower doors. (It will also come in handy for doing the windows when you do spring cleaning.)

- Teach family members to remove hair from the drain after each shower.

- Request that family members hang up towels that can be used another time.

- Keep a hamper in the bathroom for laundry. Wet towels go directly to the laundry room.

share the love—and the chores

Traditionally, women have always carried the major responsibilities for the household—even when they work in jobs outside the home. While studies show that men today are doing more around the home than their fathers, they still do only about one-third of the shopping and about 15 percent of the laundry. It's time for a change. Unless a woman lives alone, there is absolutely no reason why only she should be doing household chores. Life smiles on the couple or the family where everyone pitches in.

As for children, giving them household chores teaches responsibility. Since today's parents work so hard at creating an enriched world for their children, expecting some help around the house is a fair trade. Remind them that a few minutes of effort on their part will free all family members for time for a family bike ride or another pleasurable type of family activity.

Chores can be divided based on time, talent, interest, and even pickiness or priorities—the person who cares the most about having first-rate produce ought to be the one who stops by the farmers' or fruit market, and the one who is interested in the yard should mow the lawn. Otherwise, try these methods to reduce household friction.

Developing a Chore-Sharing System That Works

- *Agree on the goal.* Is "good enough" good enough, or does one of you need some part of the house to be "excellent?" Define or show

sanity saver

HIRE SOMEONE TO HELP YOU

Free time and your own sanity may be more worthwhile than your hard-earned money, so consider hiring help. You may decide you need someone weekly, bimonthly, monthly, or on an as-needed basis for bigger jobs like carpet or window washing or cleaning out the garage.

- To locate good help, ask friends for referrals or check online ads, classified ads, or the Yellow Pages under "house cleaning."

- If you're hiring from an agency, the agency should have done a background check. The employees also tend to be bonded.

- For cleaning, consider using a team service. The advantage to hiring a team is that with only an hour's disruption, a group of workers can blast through your household and be gone. They also tend to arrive with supplies—ranging from their own vacuums to cleansers—meaning that there are no expectations for you to run out for a new vacuum bag or floor cleaner if they run out.

examples of your standards. If you want the sheets folded a certain way or the kitchen counters left with a certain degree of order, do it once yourself as a demonstration.

- *Let everyone have some say in the chores he or she takes on.* Everyone has preferences. If Billy works nights, then perhaps he should be in charge of taking out the garbage and recycling the night before the appropriate pickup on his way to work. And if one person really enjoys cooking, let him or her be in charge of the meals; someone else can do the dishes.

- *Teach how to do a chore.* Whether it's your spouse or your child who expresses ignorance about laundry or about going to the grocery store, take time to offer helpful instruction. Go through the process with them once so that you can teach the way you'd like the chore done. (To someone who has never sorted laundry into darks and lights, this can actually be a somewhat baffling process.)

■ *Post a schedule daily, weekly, or monthly so that everyone is reminded of who does what when.* Children may respond best to chore charts where they can earn stars toward a small reward. (Paying children for major chores like cleaning out the garage is fine, but don't pay for smaller tasks that need to be done regularly.)

■ *Insist that chores be done regularly.* Some people like to do chores when they are "in the mood." This may work for occasional tasks like cleaning out the linen closet, but in general, it's best to get the regularly recurring chores on a schedule—and do them no matter what your mood. Once a chore is complete, you'll feel a new sense of satisfaction.

■ *Trade chores every month.* If you care more about cleanliness than your partner does, trading chores will ensure that you have an opportunity to deep clean some parts of the house now and then.

---

time  booster

FASTER CHORES

■ *Faster garbage fillers.* Keep extra bags at the bottom of the trash bin so that when you pull out one bag and take it off, there is a new one in the bottom.

■ *Faster plant watering.* If you have more than a plant or two, taking care of them can demand a lot of time. There are now products that will keep your plants moist and fresh for up to a month at time. Stop by a garden center and ask for information.

■ *Faster television program recording.* If you have a digital video recorder, set your system for a season pass to record your favorite programs every week, so you needn't reset each time.

- *Get in sync.* For major cleaning, some families—or couples—prefer to work at the same time. For example, one cleans the kitchen and bathrooms, while the other vacuums the bedrooms. If kids are working alongside you, state that everything must be completed before anyone leaves the house. (If you work together on Saturday mornings, perhaps everyone can go to the park or to the movies in the afternoon.) This system provides an added incentive for everyone to work quickly so that they can finish and go out to have fun.

- *Create team spirit.* Let all family members issue "tickets" for messy areas of common rooms. The person with the fewest tickets by the end of the month gets a week off from his or her chores.

- *Create a plan B.* If one person is traveling or ill or has a very busy week, how will that person's chores get done?

- *Identify areas that need improvement.* If you find you are constantly picking up the slack for your partner or one of the kids, point out what is bothering you. If they just don't understand when you ask them to empty the dishwasher in the evening so that no one has to deal with it in the morning, for example, then discuss with them another chore that they might be able to do more successfully. You should not have to absorb their job because they aren't doing it properly.

- *Compliment all honest efforts.* Even if it's not done perfectly, resist the urge to re-do. At some point, remember that it may be worth lowering your standards—after all, do you want to spend your Saturday nights at home cleaning or at the movies with the family?

spring cleaning made simple

Unfortunately, our homes need more than a once-over now and then. Dirt builds up in corners; spiders take up residence in cobwebbed corners; mold grows in showers, which is not good for anyone with allergies or asthma. When a deep cleaning is necessary, you can hire a cleaning service to do the whole thing—or to at least help out with something like window cleaning.

If you decide to do the entire job yourself, first go around the house and make a list of quickie projects, medium-length projects, or projects that are going to take a lot of time or muscle power. This list will help you select projects based on how much time you have on any given weekend. You will find that some tasks, like cobweb removal, take only a few minutes. And before you start any cleaning job, you'll need to gather the right tools, such as an all-purpose cleaner or disinfectant, glass cleaner, nonabrasive cleanser for the bathroom, sponge, cleaning cloths, old toothbrush, vacuum, and a bucket and mop.

Here are some of the chores that should go on your expanded spring cleaning list.

- Declutter closets and storage areas.

- Vacuum heating, air-conditioning, and clothes dryer vents and the refrigerator coils. (Removing dust from these places makes a big difference in efficiency.)

- Dust light fixtures and ceiling fans to clean out the bugs.

- Wash or vacuum along baseboards and spot clean the walls.

- Launder all the bedding—blankets, bed pads, and so on. If your washer isn't big enough, drop these off at a Laundromat. You can quickly freshen the pillows by tossing them in the dryer on the air cycle.

- Launder throw rugs.

- Clean window treatments. Launder the washable ones and vacuum blinds and the tops of shades. A dryer sheet also serves as a good way to wipe down Venetian blinds.

- Consider using a professional service for window and carpet cleaning.

9

the kitchen

The kitchen is a vital room in every household, and somehow we all find ourselves spending a lot of time there. Consider which of these descriptions sounds the most like you.

- *Hearth Tender*: spends a lot of time in the kitchen because he or she has a family and the tasks are unending.

- *Cook or Baker*: spends a lot of time in the kitchen because he or she loves cooking or baking.

- *Passerby*: spends as little time as possible on food preparation, but often is in the kitchen reading the newspaper, writing a list, or talking on the phone.

Regardless of whether you are a Hearth Tender, a Cook, or a Passerby, your goals are similar, because you need to take a good look at your kitchen and be sure it offers you a safe haven from the rest of the world. Whether or not you're a cook, most of us find that the kitchen can be a cozy spot to welcome in friends or to just enjoy reading the newspaper while eating a meal. This analysis usually requires reevaluating the physical space and then setting some limits for the way you use the kitchen.

Once some chores are done, your kitchen time actually can be quite restful—with some quiet time just for you.

Throughout the years, I have seen some spectacular kitchens. Often, my clients live in new homes, and their kitchens are huge. At the blueprint stage, this probably seems like a great idea—lots of space for cooking projects and lots of room for extra people. In actual practice, there is such a thing as the "too big" kitchen. One client wanted help streamlining her meal preparation process, but there was a limit to how much I could help her because there was nearly twenty-five feet between her various workstations. No matter how we planned it, she had a lot of steps to cover just to get from refrigerator to counter and then from counter to oven. And the kitchen table was another thirty feet beyond the main work area. Make no mistake—it was a beautiful kitchen. It just wasn't that practical for a one-person cooking operation.

Here are some steps you can take to ensure that your kitchen works for you.

the time-saving kitchen

No matter what your circumstance, there are two keys to a kitchen that functions well.

1. *Clutter-free counters.* It goes without saying that your counters should not hold yesterday's mail, today's schoolwork, and tomorrow's items that you have laid out to return to the store. And while it may seem convenient to keep your blender or mixer out on the counter, all it really does is create clutter—something to work around and something that has to be cleaned around. Take a look around your kitchen and keep on the counters only the items you use regularly. (Some people may actually use a blender every day, but if you don't, put it away.) If your counters are quite cluttered, you may need to devote a Saturday morning to cleaning off and reorganizing them. And always remember, tossing out is a perfectly acceptable option.

2. *Convenient work and storage areas.* I will always feel that my most functional kitchen was a tiny one in my first apartment. The reason it worked so well was that I had everything I needed nearby.

Although most of us today have larger kitchen spaces than I had then, the same principle holds true: keep dishes and implements near where you will use them. A cutting board and knives should be stored near the sink so that you can cut vegetables and quickly toss the waste. A kitchen for someone who likes to bake will have storage for measuring cups, flour, sugar, and other ingredients right near where you use the mixer.

proper storage equals greater efficiency

Being able to put your hands on what you need—from the right pan to the extra bag of flour—when you need it, will save time. Here are tips to better organize your pantry area.

- *Evaluate your primary food storage area.* If you fear opening the door or the cupboard because of what may fall out on you, then it's time to organize.

- *Make items accessible.* How well can you see what you have? (Be sure the juicer and the silver teapot aren't taking up valuable space.) If you can't locate the extra jar of peanut butter, there's little sense in buying it ahead of time.

- *Go through the pantry shelf by shelf and remove what you now realize you'll never use.* Check the expiration dates. Any foodstuff that is still good but you don't want can be donated to a shelter.

- *Establish categories.* Organize by category such as baking needs, salad dressings and condiments, mixes, pasta, and so forth.

- *Expand the space with organizers.* Wire drawers and expanding wire racks will increase your storage capacity.

- *Maximize storage space.* If your pantry area is in a closetlike space, buy a back-of-the-door organizer that can provide storage for small items (containers of bouillon, box of matches, tea, gelatin, cupcake holders, and so on).

- *Consolidate and clarify.* Everything that comes in awkward or space-hogging boxes or bags—pasta, cereal, chips—should be

sanity saver

FAMILY RESPONSIBILITIES

1. *Ask for and expect help.* It goes without saying that spouses or roommates should do their fair share—and if they aren't around to help with grocery shopping or meal prep, make certain they either take on clean-up responsibilities or absorb some other household chores to compensate for what you do in the kitchen. While assigning tasks to children as young as three or four requires a fair amount of supervision, showing them how to tear lettuce for a salad or to set the table at a young age will mean that by the time they are six or seven, they will be well prepared to be helpful members of the family.

2. *Set rules for yourself and others.* Because the kitchen is the hub of most homes, there is a great tendency to drop things off in the kitchen on the way in or out of the house. Think through how you misuse the room, and create new rules and systems for yourself and your family. Resist using the kitchen as a dumping ground. You may need to invest in a small table that you place near your most often used door (preferably not in the kitchen) or establish a spot elsewhere in the house for some of the items you've been depositing in the kitchen.

poured into transparent bulk plastic containers that store food compactly and permit you to see what's inside.

- *Alphabetize your spices.* It sounds compulsive, but it's actually very helpful.

refrigerator and freezer

You can also create order out of chaos in the refrigerator and freezer.

- Go through the refrigerator at least every two weeks. Wipe shelves and toss what you don't need (the gift jam, the leftover ingredient for a recipe you tried long ago). This way, not only will you find what you're looking for, but you'll notice when you're running low on a staple item.

- Arrange foods by category. Keep condiments on the door. Keep leftovers in one section (date the item as you put it in) to help you find and use them.

- Put fruits and vegetables in the refrigerator's produce bins.

- Leave eggs in the original carton to maintain freshness; keep meats on the coldest shelf; store leftovers in airtight containers to increase shelf life.

- Organize the freezer into categories as well. You can separate by serving size (single serving or family meals) as well as by content such as soups and side dishes. Date and label all items. Also, keep a list of what you have stored in the freezer. Knowing what you have will shorten your shopping trips and knowing what extras you've frozen will expand your meal offerings.

dishes, glassware, and kitchen miscellany

When reorganizing, clear only one shelf at a time, then clean and restock it properly.

- Store glasses and dishes near the dishwasher to make it easy to unload.

- Nest pots and pans; stack lids nearby.

- Store china, crystal, and silver separately. Do you have space in the dining area?

- Keep cooking utensils near the cooktop and working areas. They can be placed handle-side down in a big pitcher or a sturdy vase for maximum convenience.

- Stash aprons, dish towels, and pot holders in a drawer.

- Fill a basket with napkins to keep near the table.

other helpful ideas

If you look hard enough, you'll find many unexpected ways to save time and space in your kitchen.

- Consider having an instant hot water system installed. It saves time in making hot drinks and even boiling water for pasta.

- Cut the trips to the garage or the basement by building recycling bins into your kitchen cabinet.

- Take a look at your cookbooks. If you are like most of my clients, you have every cookbook that was ever given to you—many of which have never been opened. Weed out! And if you have a cookbook that you use for only one or two favorite recipes, photocopy those recipes, place them in a binder or paste them onto recipe cards, and toss the cookbook.

- Maintain a folder for recipe clippings from magazines and newspapers. If you try a recipe and like it, paste it on a card and file it. Otherwise, throw it out.

- What's in your junk drawer? Everyone has one, but these drawers need to be gone through now and then. Remove the items that are never going to be fixed, the coupons that expired a year ago, and the scissors that have been replaced by ones that actually cut. Even a junk drawer can be made to be quite handy.

- Keep a small tool kit in a kitchen drawer or the pantry. Having tools handy makes small repair jobs much easier.

quick-start meal suggestions

Family meal time is worth planning for, but most families can't work out sitting down together seven nights a week. Create a realistic schedule for what nights you can be together and plan meals accordingly.

- Develop five meals you can fix in less than thirty minutes. Then stock your cabinets with those ingredients so that you've always got them on hand. One working mother of three limits her weekday cooking to items that have no more than three ingredients.

- Dovetail tasks. If you're making vegetables as a side dish on Monday, cut up extra for Tuesday's stir-fry.

- Cook two (or more) meals at one time. On Sunday evening, fix a roast or a big turkey breast that you can use as the main ingredient for meals for the rest of the week. Or on a cold winter weekend, staying in and making soup or lasagna can be very satisfying, particularly if you make extra to freeze. (Freeze everything by family or personal portions. Label and date.)

- Cook double batches of rice and keep extra in the refrigerator or freezer. (Refrigerate if using within the week; freeze for up to six months.)

- Having chicken? Debone it for leftovers while it's still warm.

- Look for additional ways to cut corners. For example, you can skip cooking lasagna noodles in advance if you add a little extra liquid to the baking stage of lasagna making. Just layer the uncooked lasagna noodles in the pan the way you would cooked ones and be certain that they are submerged in sauce. Check periodically and add sauce if necessary.

- Order in or eat out now and then. At least once a month, you deserve a night off, and you can save up to two hours of prep and cleaning time by letting someone else do the work.

quick cleaning

You'd be surprised at how far a little forethought and prep work can go when it comes to keeping a kitchen clean.

- Reduce time on cleanup by spreading waxed paper out across your work surface. Simply pick up the paper once your work is complete.

- Line pans with foil before cooking. Let it cool after the pan comes out of the oven, then peel off and toss away. (The cost of the foil is less than the cost of the water and soap it would take to scrub off cooked-on food.)

- Doing a lot of cooking? Fill the sink with hot, soapy water, and place the pots, pans, and dishes in the sink immediately after using. This keeps your counters free and saves time on dishwashing. If food is still stuck, try one of the following remedies:

    Really stubborn food may require reheating the pan on the stove with enough water (with vinegar added) to cover the food that is stuck. Use a wooden spoon to loosen the food; cool the pan and then wash normally.

Sprinkle a layer of baking soda over the food, then add enough water to create a paste. Let it soak overnight. Wipe clean the next morning.

Soak dishes in soapy water, then rinse in a capful of vinegar and hot water to remove the excess grease and soap.

- Do the dishes after every meal. The longer dishes sit, the harder they are to clean—and if you really don't have time to wash them, at least put them in the sink to soak.

- Clean up spills in the oven and microwave and on the stove immediately. If you miss something on any of these types of heat surfaces, the food will bake on and the surface will be difficult to clean. The solution? Put a bowl of water in the microwave or oven and heat it. The moisture will loosen any baked-on dirt covering the walls of either type of oven.

- Speed counter cleanup. Keep a mixture of ammonia and water in a spray bottle under your sink. A spritz of the solution and a quick sponge wipe will leave a nongreasy clean surface.

lunch

Organize lunches for the next day when you're in the kitchen preparing or cleaning up from dinner. (Perhaps there is a great television show that you can watch while you pack the lunch.)

Ideally, children should help. The lunches will be packed in less time, and eventually, the kids will be capable of taking care of this task themselves. To pack lunches for school or the office, create a system that makes these meals easy to prepare.

- Establish a cabinet for lunch bags and drinks.

- Designate a basket to hold prepackaged foods (snack bars and so forth) and single servings of pretzels or crackers. (Save money by packing your own personal portion sizes in small plastic bags on Sunday nights.)

- Dedicate a drawer or a shelf in the refrigerator for yogurt, string cheese, celery, and grapes so these snacks are easy to add to your lunch.

■ Let young children help with the preparation; have older children pack their own lunches as part of their household responsibilities.

breakfast and snacks

If mornings are crazy at your house, consider an occasional brown-bag breakfast. Put a banana, a breakfast bar, or a box of cereal, and a juice box in a bag with a napkin. The kids can then eat breakfast on the school bus (if allowed) or in the car.

Once the children are home from school—and hungry—you can save time by preparing snacks ahead of time.

Fix snack bags of finger food—fruit, carrots, or pretzel mix—so when the kids want a snack, they don't have to interrupt you. Keep a small pitcher of milk or juice in the refrigerator for your children to fill glasses from.

the kitchen office

Even if you have a home office, most people need to establish a family center in the kitchen. A bulletin board, an oversized family wall calendar (see chapter 2), and a place for paper and writing implements, rubber bands, scissors, stamps, sticky-backed notes, a tape dispenser, a small calculator, a tape measure, and a ruler will get you started. In addition, you'll want the following.

■ The telephone placed conveniently.

■ A shelf to hold the phone directory and your address book.

■ A bulletin board for current information such as invitations, dated events, and schedules.

■ Colored markers. Designate a specific color for each family member, and write on the family calendar each person's events in the appropriate color.

groceries: buying and putting away

Even if you live alone, spend a few minutes each week planning out what you want to eat for the upcoming days. Families need full menu plans, while a single person can save extra trips to the store by knowing how much yogurt or how many meals are likely to be eaten at home the following week. Here are tips for managing grocery shopping and storage.

■ Make a list of all the everyday dishes you like and be sure to have the ingredients for those recipes on hand at all times.

■ Create a fast-pass grocery list that lists categories of items you might possibly need in the same order as your store's layout. Enter all your basics into the computer and print out copies so that you can keep a supply in the kitchen. Family members can then circle any basics needed for that week and handwrite any specialty items you'd like to buy for a specific recipe.

■ Put items on the list when you are low on them, not when you are out. Keep your list and a pencil in the kitchen so that it will be easy to note items down when you think of them.

■ Don't shop piecemeal. Try to stock up on all nonperishables and staples once a week (or if you can, visit one of the money-saving superstores and stock up once a month). A midweek stop at the store for milk and fruit should get you through until the next big shop.

■ Consider using one of the Internet shopping and delivery services. You fill out a form online regarding items you need. The store pulls the items and arranges to deliver them within a reasonable window of time. That way you're not stuck at home for hours waiting for your groceries to arrive.

■ Specialty items are now available online, so if you're looking for a special spice or artisanal cheeses or Swedish pearl sugar, try looking online first. Simply type what you're looking for into your favorite search engine, and moments later you'll have a number of prices, vendors, and shipping times to choose from.

■ Clear out the refrigerator before you go to the store so that you'll have space for incoming groceries.

■ If you do the shopping yourself, try to go at off hours. Let your spouse put the kids to bed while you go to the store alone. There are so many twenty-four-hour grocery stores that evening shopping is now a viable option, and shelves are well-stocked and the crowds are smaller than during the day.

■ Ask family members to help. A spouse or a teenager can do the grocery shopping almost as well as you can. Teach the methods for selecting fruits and vegetables so that you'll have the quality you want. Even little ones can be shown how to help at the store by picking out items on lower shelves. (It will slow you down initially during the training period, but it will save you time later on.)

■ If you have a babysitter for the kids who has down time while they are at school, delegate at least some of your grocery shopping to her. (Make it part of the initial job description.)

■ Buy some food ready-made. Although prepared foods are a bit more expensive, many people like to have a night or two when they don't have to make dinner. Whether it's deboned chicken, precut vegetables, chopped garlic, or fully prepared casseroles, the time you save in food prep may make the cost worthwhile.

■ At the grocery store, buy items in the form you will need them: prewashed lettuce; shredded or grated cheese; precut vegetables; boneless, skinless chicken; and so on.

■ Buy in multiples. Start with at least two of everything and store the extras in out-of-kitchen areas such as the basement or closet. When you open the last roll of paper towels, add it to your shopping list.

■ When you pack your groceries at the store, divide the nonperishables and frozen foods from the fresh food to save time unpacking at home.

■ Keep a few laundry baskets in the back of the car so that you can load them with the grocery bags for the ride home. Items won't roll around as much, and you'll be able to bring the groceries into the house more quickly because you can bring in the full basket.

■ As you unpack the groceries, organize as you go. This will simplify and speed you along at dinnertime. (Traditional meal prep time— late afternoon or early evening—is usually the most hectic time of day, so the less you have to do at that time, the easier the prep will be.) If you buy larger quantities of meat than you'll eat in a week, divide, repackage, and freeze appropriate-size portions to use later on. Wash fruits and vegetables you expect to use within the next day or so, and wipe off individual containers of water and soda. If you snack on carrots or celery, these can be cut up and stored in water in the refrigerator so you can grab and go.

10

express laundry

*D*oing the laundry is one of life's necessities—and keeping up with it regularly is the best way to keep laundry from becoming a must-do crisis item. One of my recent clients, a single working mom, found that she was doing laundry after midnight. I showed her there were other ways to get laundry done without having it dominate her home time. Another client refused to allow other family members to help her because she thought she could do it "better" than they could, until I pointed out that with today's automatic washers and clothing made of the new types of fabric, it really was possible to train other family members to do it as well as she could. Also consider it your duty: you owe that type of training to your children! When I was helping my daughter move into her college dorm room one year, we passed by the dorm's laundry room and overheard a girl on her cell phone, saying, "Okay, Mom. I've put in the soap. What do I do now?"

We all need to learn to do laundry at some point, and if you teach everyone your methods now, you'll benefit because they'll be able to help you before they move out.

A well-organized system and a schedule that works are the two primary keys to tackling laundry in a minimum of time.

laundry for apartment dwellers

If you live in an apartment, doing laundry is more complicated than it is for homeowners who have a washer and dryer only steps away.

- Consider stackables. You need access to water pipes and a closet or some wall space to add these to your apartment, but the time savings of being able to toss in a load without running to the building's basement can be considerable. (Check with the building management to see if there are any rules regarding adding machines.)

- Consider dropping off your laundry at a laundry service in your neighborhood.

- The fewer times you have to wash the laundry, the more time you will save. If investmenting in another week's worth of underwear will let you stretch doing laundry to only twice a month, then purchase what you need to minimize your time in front of a washer and dryer.

- Alternate with a friend or neighbor—you do laundry for both of you one week; he or she does it the following week.

---

mini vacation

HAVE ONE WITH THE LAUNDRY

If you have to go out to a self-service laundry or if slow elevators in your building make it more efficient for you to sit down near the washing machines in your building, create a pleasant "vacation" for yourself. Save up on pleasure reading, or consider whether you have any portable hobbies such as knitting that could be taken with you and pursued during this time. If you find a leisure activity that you look forward to working on during laundry time, you'll soon wish you could do the laundry more frequently!

- If doing your laundry yourself is your best option, experiment to find the slow time in your building so that once you've set aside the time, you'll be able to get machines. Weekends tend to be the busiest, but you may find that before your early run on Saturday mornings you can beat the crowd. Colleges are adding Web cams so that students can easily check to see if machines are available, or to see if it's time to change from washer to dryer. Perhaps your building would consider adding this type of option.

- Have the right supplies to make your trip easy and efficient.

  Invest in a wheeled cart that is a good size to hold your laundry and that will fit in the elevator.

  Stockpile quarters or go to the bank and exchange bills for a few rolls of quarters.

  Purchase smaller containers for the detergent so you don't need to lug a big jug with you. As soon as you get home, be sure to refill it if necessary.

establishing a laundry system in your home

Laundry should be a job that takes minutes, not one that consumes several hours, and part of accomplishing that goal is creating a convenient system. A generation ago, it used to be common practice to put the washer and dryer in the basement. Today, busy families are realizing that it's far easier to get the laundry done if the washer and dryer are near the kitchen or the bedrooms. If you have the opportunity to renovate, consider what would be most convenient for you. Otherwise, here are some tips to help you reduce the time you spend on the laundry.

- Label family members' clothing right after purchase. Use permanent markers to write initials, or develop a family dot system—a different color dot for each person.

- Each family member should have a hamper in his or her bathroom or bedroom. Keep a stain stick or spray (a prewash product) near each individual hamper, and teach everyone to treat stains soon after they occur. For tougher stains—such as those on baby clothes—soak the garment as soon as it's removed.

- If it isn't dirty, don't clean it. Teenage girls are particularly good at tossing an item into the laundry because they tried it on. Let your kids know that an item has to be worn in order to qualify for being be washed.

- Teach family members to empty pockets and turn things right side out as they remove the clothing. (Some dark items wash best if turned inside out, so point out to them any items where the inside-out method applies.)

- Show family members how to shake out their socks before tossing them into the hamper. Socks should not go into the wash wadded into a ball, because they won't get clean. And at some point, it will cost you time when you find the socks still soggy and wet as they come out of the dryer.

- If a hem has pulled loose or a button is lost, take care of it when you notice it. Don't put the piece of clothing in the wash (or back in the closet) until you've taken care of the repair.

- Eliminate most hand laundry by putting delicate items in zippered mesh bags to be washed on the gentle cycle.

- Get family members to bring their own clothes to the laundry area. If they fail to do so, then their laundry just won't get washed.

- Purchase a laundry area hamper with two sections. That way everyone can separate his or her own clothing into "darks" and "lights" and all that is left to you is loading the washer.

---

mini  vacation

HAVE ONE WHILE IRONING

Most of us have to iron now and then, so record one of your favorite television programs to watch while ironing. You'll get a major task out of the way while doing something pleasant that you may not otherwise have time for.

- Teach teenagers to do the laundry. While it may still make sense to maintain a family laundry system with everyone's clothing washed together so that you can separate lights and darks, making teens responsible for their own beach towels or sports uniforms will save you time. And remember, it is good preparation for college and later in life—remember the girl on the cell phone in the laundry room whom I described at the beginning of the chapter?

speedy sock management

Sorting and dealing with socks wastes time, so follow these hints to make sock organization easier.

- Every family member should have a different kind of sock for easy identification and to reduce sorting and pairing time.

- Put socks in a mesh bag to keep them from getting lost in the corners of big sheets or clinging to other clothing. (If family members wear similar socks, purchase extra mesh bags and make each person responsible for sorting his or her own socks into the appropriate bag.)

- If socks do get separated, establish a bin in the laundry room for odd socks. At some point, the pair will be reunited.

folding and putting away laundry

Washing clothes is only half the battle. These tips will make folding and putting away laundry a snap.

- Take clothing out of the dryer when it stops. A quick shake or a smooth folding will mean no or reduced ironing time.

- If a piece of clothing has been left to sit and become wrinkled, put it and a dryer sheet in the dryer on low heat for about ten minutes. This will reduce or eliminate ironing. You might also try hanging things in the bathroom while you shower; the wrinkles may steam out that way.

- Get everyone to pitch in with folding. Each person should also be responsible for picking up his or her clean clothing from the laundry room and putting it away.

- Keep a lint brush near where you generally fold the laundry to pick up any lint or stray pet hairs.

- An additional time-saver is to fold sheets lengthwise. When you make the bed, you'll find it goes more quickly because you can properly position and unfold the sheets.

11

household paper management

*M*ost homes I visit have at least one area where paper clutter overtakes the space—and a good number of homes are simply drowning in paper. After all, it arrives in your household every day, and if you don't find an effective and efficient way to deal with it, it soon costs you time—for example, searching for the phone bill that is now overdue, wondering what you did with the tickets for the game, or looking for the retrieval stub for your shoes that you left for repair.

I'm often called in because of some disaster or another: one couple missed the opera because they had misplaced the tickets; one family missed their flight—they had the tickets, they just never checked the date and went to the airport a day late—and too late as far as the airline was concerned. Clients have been assessed finance charges because they never can find their credit-card bills to pay them on time; parents have ripped up households looking for permission slips; kids have been reduced to tears because they can't find the book report "they put *there* last night"; and countless clients have lost their to-do lists, but that's another story.

quick  start

GET ORGANIZED

Every single piece of paper in the house—from bills to shopping lists, from clip-and-save recipes to letters—fits into one of four categories: to pay, to do, to file, to answer.

Set up an office mail tray for each. This will reduce paper buildup and end time-consuming paper searches.

You'll have more time for you if you find great systems for managing your household papers.

mail

Although more and more of us are relying on e-mail (a bit more on that in a moment) as our preferred method of communication, it has done little to slow incoming snail mail. There seem to be more catalogs than ever, bills and solicitations still often come by mail, and, of course, we all have magazines we enjoy. One client was quite horrified when her mail carrier arrived with a stack of her family's mail that stood at least eighteen inches high—and that was just for one day. As a result, the mail still needs to be sorted carefully and thoroughly every day.

mail management

If you create an organized method for processing the mail, you will notice an instant difference in your home and desk clutter.

- "Sort and toss" is my rule for mail management. The mail arrives six days per week, so Monday to Saturday your first pass through the mail stack should be sorting the mail by family member. Then quickly go through your stack, tossing as much as you can to avoid buildup. You might love a particular catalog company, but if you're particularly busy that week, toss out the catalog. They'll send you another soon enough.

- Personal letters (if you still get them!) can be opened first—that's human nature. Unless you need the envelope for the return address, toss it and write on the top of the letter what happens next: "answer" or "file." Then leave it for the next family member to read.

- Bills and bank statements should be opened and given a once-over in case there is a mistake. Circle the due date or mark it on the envelope and then put it in a to-pay folder or drawer.

- Solicitations for donations to causes that interest you should be put aside with the bills. You can take care of all payments at one time. By paying your bills first, you'll also be better prepared to realistically assess how generous to be.

- Invitations directed to you alone should be responded to right away. Phone, e-mail, or mail back your reply, and write the information on your calendar. Note the address as well, or write down where you are filing the invitation and the driving directions so that you'll be able to find them later.

- Catalogs can save shopping time, but if a stack builds up in your house, then they are just one more thing to manage. Try to go through the ones that interest you on a daily basis, and if you can't manage that, make a deal with yourself to do it at least once a week. (If you haven't looked through a saved catalog after a week, toss it.) You can phone in your order or process it online. (The online systems are so easy now that they make phone ordering seem very time consuming.)

e-mail management

Work-related e-mail will be discussed in part four of this book, but I am well aware that personal e-mail is beginning to consume people's home time in the way that regular mail used to. Here are tips to better manage your e-mail.

- Establish a regular time to review and read your e-mail.

- Set a time limit for how long you want to spend at the computer—fifteen to thirty minutes in the morning and at night is a good guideline. Between the joke e-mails, instant messaging, and the forwarded links that are sent around, you can find yourself spending endless amounts of time at the computer if you don't remain conscious of what you are doing. (If you are an "addict," buy a wind-up timer and keep it by your computer so that you can limit yourself.)

- Like paper mail, e-mail needs to be sorted. Create folders and move any e-mails you want to save into the appropriate folder. Consider a "family" folder, a "to answer" folder for the e-mail messages you don't have time to respond to, and folders for any other topics.

- Be cautious about how much you sign up for online. Just as you can oversubscribe to magazines or catalogs, you can oversubscribe on the Internet. If you're really interested in a subject, then sign up for an online newsletter. If you're not certain you are that interested, put the Web site in your favorites lineup. Then you can check out the updates when you have time, but you won't be bombarded by e-mail messages.

reduce incoming mail, e-mail, and phone solicitations

The following strategies will help you escape the burden of paper and electronic mail and hold those pesky telemarketers at bay.

- To reduce incoming mail, write to: Mail Preference Service, Direct Marketing Association, P.O. Box 9008, Farmingdale, NY 11735-9008. Provide the service with various forms of your name, "John," "John A.," "J.A.," and so forth) and ask to be removed from mailing lists. It won't totally solve your problem, but it will help.

- Write directly to companies asking to be removed from their lists.

- When you send in a donation, order things by mail, or sign up to receive literature, always look to see if there is a box you can check off to indicate that you don't want to receive other solicitations.

- Opt out of some e-mail solicitations. Because there is so much unregulated spam, this will not be a cure-all. However, in the spirit of "everything helps," go to www.dmaconsumers.org/consumers/optoutform. If Internet mail systems become more carefully controlled, perhaps this registration will be more effective than it is now.

- Unwanted phone solicitations are also annoying. Sign up on the "no call" list at www.donotcall.gov or call 1-888-832-1222.

time ( ) booster

MAGAZINES

Because I've been in so many homes that have stacks and stacks of unread magazines, I've created four rules of magazine management.

1. Most people don't have time to read a magazine on the day it arrives, so it's okay to designate a place on a side table or a magazine rack where you keep unread magazines.

2. Set aside time to go through these magazines at least once a week. If you see an article that interests you but don't have time to read it, rip it out, staple the pages, and put it in an on-the-go reading file that you can take with you when commuting or waiting at a doctor's office. (You'll still need to be selective, or you'll have a collection of articles that you'll never get through!)

3. Be diligent about working through your magazines or keeping up with the on-the-go reading file. If you haven't read what you've saved within four to six weeks, toss it.

4. Consider magazine renewals carefully. Your interests—and the time you have available for reading—may have changed.

your files

Today, the Internet has reduced some of the need for saving papers. If you find a great article about a resort, there is little need to save it in case you ever get to take that trip, because when the time comes, you can simply go online and check out the latest information on your destination. The same thing is true for health recommendations. No need to clip and save ideas for eating heart healthy because all that advice is as near as your computer.

Most people have trouble adjusting to this new way of thinking. "You mean I really don't need to save this?" is a question I'm asked frequently. More and more of the time, I'm able to say, "No, you really don't need to save a lot of papers anymore." And, of course, the less paperwork we have to save, the less time we have to spend managing it.

That said, we all have some papers we must keep. Some are legal documents, some are personal records, and some are papers that have information we think might be hard to find elsewhere.

In most households, files can be broken into three categories:

1. *Active files.* These are ongoing projects, backup papers for your to-do list, a file for the new car you're considering buying, and so forth. Separate the to-do file into three sections: *Immediate*, handled within the week; *Coming Up*, within thirty days; and *To Review* or *Ongoing Projects*, for items you're considering (check monthly).

2. *Stored files.* This is current information that you've processed but need to hold on to. Financial files, including paid bills, insurance policies, bank statements, reports, and so forth, are an example of stored files. Personal items to store might include a child's scholastic testing, an appliance manual, a job estimate for a home project, or a sweet thank-you letter you received.

3. *Cold files.* These are items such as tax returns or legal documents that need to be kept for the long term, but you likely don't require immediate access to them. (They actually can be stored someplace cold like a basement or a garage.)

Be sure to put the following documents in a safe place that's easily accessible: bank information, car documents, education records, housing information such as rental agreements or mortgage papers, insurance policies, tax information, and medical records.

Official documents such as birth certificates, passports, legal papers, deeds, and wills should secured in a safe deposit box.

Helpful Rules for Filing

- Label all file folders. Color code as much as possible; for example, assign green files (or at least green-edged file labels) for financial documents; blue for volunteer work; and red for to-do items or active projects.

- If you're starting a new project, create a new file folder so that you don't just "pile."

- Date and note the source of every paper that you file. Also note if there is a date when you'll no longer need the paper: "Toss after _____."

- Organize within the file. Most files can be organized chronologically, and this is easy to do by slipping the most recently received paper into the front of the file.

- If you have to remove papers from a file for any length of time, leave yourself a reminder note of where you've put the removed papers. When you go to the insurance file looking for your policy and it's not there, you'll be delighted to find the reminder, noting that your spouse was reviewing something and has the policy on his desk.

- Staple together papers that belong together. Paper clips can get caught on other papers, so it's easy for an unrelated paper to attach itself to a clipped group. Staples avoid that problem.

- File regularly. Everyone needs a "to file" office tray, but be sure you process the papers on a daily or weekly basis. When filing is done in small bits of time, it is an easy task. (If you let it build up, it will overwhelm you and you just won't finish it.)

- Weed out regularly. Whenever you pull a file, take a few minutes to clean it out.

family finances made simple

Despite the fact that keeping our finances straight is one of our most important adult responsibilities, I frequently go into homes where bills, credit-card receipts, ATM slips, investment records, and bank

---

sanity  saver

DEALING WITH A BACKLOG OF PAPERS

Tackle the backlog. If you have a lot of accumulation, the pile can be overwhelming. Start by sorting through a small stack at a time. Allow a half an hour a day to sift through old papers. You'll be amazed at how much you can accomplish by setting up a systematic way of going through everything. Once you're organized, you can spend time on what really matters.

statements are spread out or tucked into surprising places. One business owner stored her invoices under her living room couch cushions—for lack of a better system.

If you open the mail and deal with these papers in a prompt and orderly fashion, you'll be able to find what you need at tax time or when you need proof that a department store bill is in error. Here's how to manage your home financial work so that you can stay on top of it.

- Be systematic. Pay your bills on time and then file what you have taken care of. Establish a system where you pay bills weekly or biweekly to avoid late fees.

- File what you must save.

- Toss what you can (see page 133 for how long to keep what).

finding time for personal finances

Whether investing for retirement, saving for college, or learning about your insurance provisions, it's important that you make time for managing your personal finances.

Managing personal finances involves two separate types of tasks:

1. The day-to-day of money management such as paying bills, making deposits, balancing the checkbook, and so forth

2. Examining the big picture and deciding how to allot your money among different types of saving instruments and investments.

When I consult with couples, I frequently recommend alternating these financial responsibilities every six months. It spreads the burden of the task equally between two people, and it provides each person with some perspective on the impact the spending has on your family income. Understanding the financial toll of eating at expensive restaurants is much clearer—and makes it easier to reset budgeting goals—if both of you have taken a turn at examining the credit-card bills and have served a stint paying them.

Day-to-Day Money Issues

- Direct-deposit your salary, social security, and other income to save time going to the bank. This also gives you access to the money in the fastest manner possible.

■ Manage money the way you shop for food—do it regularly. Bills need to be paid once or twice per month (note it on your calendar so you don't forget), and you need to devote time each week to take care of routine duties such as filling out reimbursement forms, checking online accounts, calling to dispute a billing charge, and so on.

■ Establish automatic payments for recurring bills such as mortgage payments.

■ Use an e-mail alert program to send yourself reminders on paying taxes or renewing insurance.

■ Do your banking online to help cut down on time spent writing checks and mailing bills.

■ Make a photocopy of both sides of your credit cards and leave the copy at home in a safe place. If you should ever lose any of the cards, you'll be able to call in with the necessary information.

■ List your various insurance policy numbers and social security numbers in one place. (If you carry family social security information with you, use a less-than-obvious method for noting whose number is whose, such as "Daughter #1," instead of "Julia." If your purse is stolen, you don't want to have to worry about identity theft for all family members.)

Looking at the Big Picture, Financially Speaking

■ Schedule an annual review of your finances. If you are part of a couple, the two of you should sit down together, possibly with a financial adviser. Tax time is a logical opportunity for this type of review. Reevaluate your financial goals, examine any changes in income, and look at your savings and investments to be certain they are accomplishing the goals you set.

■ Schedule a few hours once a month for dealing with some of the big-picture items that may require attention before your annual review: researching where to invest for college, comparison shopping for insurance, updating a will, and so on.

banking and bill paying online

In a recent study conducted by the Pew Internet and American Life Project, today more than 53 million people—or about 44 percent of all

Internet users—check their bank accounts online. And at major financial institutions, nearly half of all customers pay their bills online. If you haven't entered the Internet banking age, you may want to do so now—it can be convenient, save time, and reduce household paper clutter.

Here are some tips for using online banking.

- Bookmark the bank's address in your browser. Fake Web sites have been set up to capture anyone who makes a slight typo when entering an address, so you may find that you have accidentally arrived on a forged bank site—and you don't want to attempt to enter your account number and password there.

- Look for good security.

  Ask about data encryption.

  There should be a written guarantee to protect account holders from losses caused by online fraud.

  There should be an automatic lockout if a password is entered incorrectly more than three or four times.

  There should be an automatic logout if you are not active on the site for a certain amount of time.

  Read up on the latest security methods. Some banks are using a photo security method (you click on a photo that is assigned to your account); others are issuing key ring electronic tokens that reveal to you a new, one-use-only password for your account every sixty seconds. This security measure is a big deterrent against anyone hacking into your account, and while it sounds complex, it is actually very user friendly. When you need to access your account, simply check your key ring for the current password and enter it on the site for immediate access to your account. Many banks also provide an alert each time there is activity on the account so if you haven't been active when the bank notifies you, you can contact the bank immediately to halt any transactions by a hacker.

- See if your online bill-paying method can be integrated with the electronic accounting program you're using, if applicable. That way your bills are paid and all bookkeeping issues are resolved with a single entry.

- One warning about online banking and bill paying: if there is a dispute, it is a little more difficult to resolve than if you have created a paper trail that can prove your case. By the same token, most banks set a limit on customer losses.

- Some companies permit you to pay bills online at their Web site. There you can check the amount you owe, and you can pay either by credit card or by authorizing a deduction from your bank account. If you use your credit card, you may still find yourself writing out a check for your credit-card bill once a month, but the online system permits you to consolidate most of your bill paying. If you authorize a deduction from your bank account, you'll need to fill out forms ahead of time that establish a system for this payment method.

In addition, when paying bills online, keep in mind the following.

- Enter all account numbers and company names exactly as they appear on your billing statements.

- Plan your payments well in advance.

- Recurring bills of the same amount can be scheduled for automatic payments. For cell phone or utility bills that can vary each month, enter the amounts in time to avoid a late payment or set up parameters so that all invoices under a certain amount can be paid automatically; the company can e-mail you for authorization on bills that run over the agreed-upon amount.

sanity saver

PROTECT YOUR ONLINE INFORMATION

Create a unique password. Most companies recommend a combination of letters and numbers. Resist using anything as obvious as your pet's name or your mother's maiden name. The best passwords are letters and symbols that require the alt key. Security experts say those passwords are 99 percent uncrackable.

■ Remember that not all companies can accept electronic payments. If you are using a bill-paying service (many banks offer them), then the service must send those businesses a check, a process that can take up to ten days. Most sites will advise you of this in advance.

■ The funds leave your account on the day the bill payment is due to be sent. Update your check register regularly to reflect these payments; otherwise you risk overdrawing your account.

documents: what to keep and for how long

The more paper you can weed out, the less time managing it will take. Unfortunately, there are certain documents we have to hang on to for legal and tax reasons. Here is what you need to know about tossing and saving.

Toss Every Month

■ ATM and bank-deposit slips. Record the needed information, and once you have checked them against your statements, toss.

■ Credit-card receipts. Check to make sure the information is correct on your statements. *File what you will need for tax purposes or possible returns*; toss the rest.

■ Sale receipts for minor purchases. Toss, unless you're self-employed and the purchase is tax deductible.

Toss after Two Years

■ Monthly bank and credit-card statements (if you don't itemize deductions).

■ Monthly or quarterly brokerage and mutual-fund statements after you've reconciled them with your year-end report.

■ Monthly mortgage statements (as long as your year-end statement is correct.)

■ Phone and utility bills, as long as you don't have a home office or deduct these expenses.

■ Paycheck stubs after you've reconciled them with your annual W-2 and 1099 forms.

Hold until Sold

- Confirmation slips for securities
- Real estate deeds
- Home improvement records
- Receipts for major purchases with replacement costs exceeding your homeowners' or renters' insurance deductible

Retain for Seven Years

- Forms W-2 and 1099
- Year-end statements from credit-card companies
- Phone and utility bills if you deduct for business expenses, have more than one home, or have moved within the last few years
- Canceled checks and receipts/statements for the following: annual mortgage interest and property taxes, deductible business expenses, child-care bills, out-of-pocket medical costs, or any other tax-deductible expense

Keep Indefinitely

- Annual tax returns
- Year-end statements from financial service companies
- Confirmation slips that list the purchase price of any investments you own
- Papers that indicate beneficiary designations

12

the holidays

There's no time like the holidays for feeling time pressured and stressed out. With an extra-long to-do list, which now includes buying presents, decorating, and entertaining, and a calendar filled with holiday obligations, it's hard to think of finding time to do anything for yourself.

As December nears and everyone's stress levels start to rise, it becomes easy to identify with my client who was so tired of "doing for" everyone else throughout the holiday month that one year she announced to her family that she was going on strike. She told them that unless everyone got together for a family meeting to divide up the holiday-related tasks, their family holiday was just not going to materialize. Her family—husband, two teens, and two preteens—did sit down with her, and not only did they agree to take over some of the jobs she had always done alone, but they also came up with some gift-giving plans that simplified the shopping process. My client later told me, "I stood up for myself, and it was the best thing I ever did."

The true ingredients for an enjoyable holiday are family and friends and having time to enjoy them. Here are some suggestions on how to find time, save time, and enjoy your holidays.

■ *Remove the "should" from the holidays.* Sit down with the friends or family members with whom you will spend the holidays and discuss what is important to each person. Try to build December's calendar with the goal of letting each person choose one activity—whether it's baking cookies together or going to a holiday movie—and then say no to the invitations or events that aren't part of the priority list everyone has decided upon. If just being with the family is what you want to do this holiday, then turn down outside invitations. You can reemerge for social interactions in January.

■ *Consider what decorating you really want to do.* Skip whatever you don't enjoy or isn't necessary.

■ *Think outside the box.* There are no rules for having a proper holiday. If your extended family or group of friends thinks that back-to-back movies followed by a big dinner of pancakes would make for a fun holiday, then go for it.

■ *Set limits.* When you were single or just a couple, it may have been possible to make the rounds to parents and in-laws on the same day. A new baby often complicates your schedule. Make a new decision— are you staying home and can they come to you? Are you going to alternate houses year to year? Decide what will work for you, and give everyone some advance warning so they'll have time to adjust.

■ *Simplify.* Instead of creating an elaborate gingerbread house this year, frost cookies together instead.

■ *Consider volunteering for your favorite charity or gathering gifts for people in need.* Although volunteering adds to your to-do list, the rewards are great, and donating your time truly exemplifies the holiday spirit. Check with nearby military bases, veteran's groups, your church, a local shelter, or a teen center to see how you can help. One family has created a tradition of working together at a soup kitchen every holiday to remind themselves of how lucky they are.

■ *Even a holiday party can be for a good cause.* Request that guests bring a wrapped toy or book for a child (marked with what it is or the age for which it is appropriate), and then donate those items to a local charity.

■ *Don't be a martyr by trying to make everything "perfect" for everyone else.* The day will be more pleasant for everyone—you especially—if you skip the part where you're so overworked that the holiday isn't fun anymore.

save time by being better organized

One surefire way to save time during the hectic holiday season is to organize seasonal supplies. You'll never have time to bake your favorite holiday cookies, for example, if you have to spend hours tearing the house apart to find Grandma's special recipe!

■ Create a holiday binder. Buy a notebook to dedicate to the holidays. This is a useful time-saver when used year after year. Buy a set of five dividers with pockets. Then dedicate a section to:

1. Holiday to-do list

2. Holiday card list

3. Holiday recipes

4. Gift ideas (catalog pages that show gift ideas, receipts for purchases, and so forth)

5. Entertaining

mini vacation

CREATE SOME QUIET TIME IN THE CHAOS

Whether it's renting a copy of *It's a Wonderful Life* or watching one of the annual holiday specials on television, include some quiet activities as part of your plans. These passive activities let you enjoy the spirit of the holiday without wearing you out the way shopping, cooking, and decorating can.

- Establish a wrap-and-mail center so that wrapping will be quick and easy. Set up a card table for the actual wrapping center and store paper, ribbon, gift tags, and tape nearby. (You'll also need easy access to boxes and packing tape if you mail your gifts.)

- Start a family blog—an Internet posting site—where you can update extended family members about your life, post photos, or exchange information. At holiday time, for example, you can save time and phone calls by posting a sign-up sheet to track who is bringing what to the family holiday gathering.

- Hire a couple of high school students to help out with anything from babysitting and gift wrapping to gift delivery or party cleanup.

- Accept (and encourage!) help. Having others pitch in will actually make the holiday more fun.

holiday time-savers

Leaving holiday tasks—from shopping to baking—to the last minute creates havoc. Stores are busier and your patience will be frayed if you wait. Here are ways to avoid holiday havoc.

- Purchase tickets for special entertainments—from a professional basketball game to the local theatrical extravaganza—well in advance. You not only create a positive plan but you assure yourself of getting the best possible seats.

- Evaluate everyone's clothing needs for the holidays. If Timmy has outgrown his blazer and Susie doesn't even own a dress, take care of those things by early December so that you don't fling open the closet only to discover that someone has nothing to wear.

- All service businesses get extra busy around holiday time, so book haircuts for family members and a grooming appointment for the dog well in advance.

- Think through general holiday food needs and clean out the freezer so that you'll have space for food-related gifts or for any holiday food that you can make ahead of time and freeze.

- Stockpile a few emergency gifts (guest soaps or specialty foods such as jellies, teas, nuts, and so forth) to have on hand for last-minute hostess gifts or as a small gift for someone you forgot.

- Keep small gift bags with your wrapping paper supply to make wrapping easier.

- Delegate some holiday responsibilities to other family members.

gift buying

Perhaps the largest source of stress during the holiday season is buying gifts for family, friends, and coworkers. It can drain your time, patience, and finances. These tips can help you manage holiday shopping while saving your sanity.

- Update your gift list. If you've always exchanged gifts with cousins but it's beginning to feel like a big burden as the kids get older, open a discussion about this (but talk to them early in the season before they get a chance to shop for you). They likely will be equally glad to simplify their own gift giving.

- Everyone worries about what to do about the people at work. If you're in a position to sway opinion, suggest that instead of exchanging gifts, you'll choose a charity to sponsor for the holidays. Everyone can donate in the form of a check or gifts to the charity instead. If you choose a children's charity where wrapped gifts are desired, ask everyone to pitch in a couple of dollars more so that you can throw a staff pizza party for getting together to wrap the gifts.

- Consider these innovative ways to reduce the gift-buying overload.

  Have two or three family members team up to buy a gift together for another family member.

  Use the draw-a-name system so that each person shops for only one other family member—but someone different each year.

  Send gift certificates for services—such as beauty or nail salons or massages—magazine subscriptions, or museum memberships. Or promise to pay for a one-hour guitar lesson or a session with a personal trainer.

Offer a personal IOU for a favor or chore you can do for the recipient, anything from an evening of babysitting to three Saturdays of errand running.

Offer tickets to a sporting event, a ballet, or a play.

Give the good old green stuff, and don't even bother to pick up a gift card. Sometimes cash is truly the most appreciated—your college student may realize it is more important to pay off his phone bill rather than have a gift card to a sporting goods store.

For friends or relatives with whom you exchange gifts, consider one appropriate family gift rather than individual gifts for each person. For example, a hammock, a board game, a jigsaw puzzle, or a gift certificate for a dinner at their favorite restaurant can be as much appreciated as smaller individual gifts for which you've shopped long and hard.

If you plan to shop for gifts, here are ways to save time.

- Work from a clear shopping list—and stick to it. Use your holiday notebook to create your to-do list. When you get home, write down what you have purchased, for whom, and where you are storing it. (There is nothing worse than realizing in a panic, "I know I bought Aunt Sadie an espresso maker, but what did I do with it?")

- Divide up the gift buying. There is no rule that says only women can buy holiday presents. Men too can go to the store or press BUY IT NOW on a Web site. And what about pooling all the sibling resources together for one gift for Mom or Dad? Working together to come up with the right idea builds family unity and lessens the holiday madness of everyone running around.

- Go online for gift ideas. Because searching at the mall for the perfect holiday gift is hard on both your spirits and your feet, there are now online services that promise to find the perfect gift for your great aunt, cousin Sue, or father. These personal shopper Web sites (like www.gifts.com or Gift Central on www.amazon.com) ask you to enter details about each recipient such as their likes and your price range. Once you've narrowed down the suggestions, you can use one of the price comparison Web sites (such as www.robo shopper.com) to run a search for the best deal.

- Shopping online or from a catalog can save you time going to the mall, but you do need to stay organized. Use your holiday binder to:

  Keep a copy of the order confirmation if you've purchased a gift online (or keep a copy of the page from the catalog if it was a phone order).

  Create a list of the gifts you've ordered, and allow space for tracking information.

  When the gift arrives, wrap it and put it away fully labeled.

- Have gifts shipped directly to recipients to save time having to take things home and pack and wrap them.

- Shop all year-round. If you see something in July that is just perfect for your mom, buy it. As the holidays near, you'll feel terrific knowing that you have a great gift—and you don't have to worry about shopping.

- For the items still on your list, start early in the day to avoid the holiday crowds and the parking headaches. You can be done before most people head out to the stores.

- Shop at small stores where more personal service may make the process easier, or try using a personal shopper at a department store who will work through your list for you.

- Buy multiples of something that seems like a terrific gift for several people or is perfect as a hostess gift. From pretty frames to specially flavored olive oils, these gifts are fun to receive and they will please a broad array of people.

- Gift-wrapping purchases at the store sometimes means having to wait for the packages to be wrapped, so try dropping off gifts while you still have other shopping to complete. Later, pick up the wrapped gifts on your way back to the car.

- Save time and money by using assorted-colored tissue paper as wrapping paper. A colorful package with a ribbon added can make for a perfectly attractive package.

- If you have to return things, don't go the day after the holiday when the stores will be absolutely packed. Hold off for a couple of days until the crowds are more manageable.

sending holiday cards

Sending holiday cards is both a thoughtful way to stay in touch with people you don't see regularly and sometimes a business necessity. Those who send cards want their wishes to arrive on time, and most of us aspire to add a personal note on many of the cards. To send cards efficiently, here are some suggestions.

Four Ways to Save Time by Planning Ahead

1. If you customarily send along a family or personal photo, keep this in mind throughout the year. A family reunion in August offers an opportunity to get a decent group shot, and you'll save time and stress in December because you won't have to get everyone dressed up and gathered in pursuit of the perfect holiday picture.

2. Create a realistic list of recipients that is meaningful. Use holiday cards as a sweet way to stay in touch with people whom you want to keep in your life. Unless you have a new baby whose photo you want to include, there is no need to send a card to people you see every day. Cut from the list the neighbors who moved away three years ago and to whom you haven't spoken since.

3. Store a copy of the list (whether e-mail addresses or street addresses) in a file or in your holiday binder. Add in any change-of-address notices you receive, any cards you send that come back as undeliverable (today's postal computers generally paste on an address correction notice), as well as any personal reminders of new acquaintances or people you know who have changed addresses. In less than an hour, you'll be able to bring your card list up to date.

4. Order stamps online to avoid waiting at the post office. At www.usps.com, you can order holiday stamps in bulk, or you can create your own stamp using a photo of your children, the new puppy, or the house you are renovating at www.photostamps.com.

Quick Cards That Save Time

- Consider e-cards. E-mailing your greetings is faster and cheaper than sending a real card. Search for "e-cards with personal photos."

Friends will be glad to see your smiling face pop up, and computer-savvy grandparents can create their own keepsake print of your family.

- Even if you want to send a paper card, you can create a custom one online. The online photo developing services all offer cards as an option, but there are also online card companies that let you choose from their nonphoto designs and greetings—they'll even mail them off for you for a price.

- If you're sending paper cards, etiquette advisers may say "hand address; don't use labels," but life is too short to get hung up on how the address appears on the envelope. A typed list that you can run through your printer onto mailing labels will save you time, and the card recipient will simply be delighted to hear from you. (If you are technophobic or decide you absolutely must address by hand, do it while watching a movie, or consider hiring a teen to do the addressing for you.)

- If you enjoy writing holiday letters, do so on the computer. You can create one letter with details of your vacation, your dad's health, and where your son is going to college, but then you can personalize the letters you send by writing opening and closing paragraphs that directly relate to the recipient.

holiday entertaining

Although we get bogged down in the decorating and shopping and cooking of the holidays, the true spirit of holiday time is getting together. So whether the party is at your house or your parents' or your best friend's, here are some ways to make it manageable.

- If you invite a big gang every holiday, consider having all or part of the meal catered. If spending time together is what's important, there is no shame in having the food prepared by someone else.

- Accomplish a task while socializing. Instead of having people in for lunch or dinner, invite friends or family to a baking or a wrapping party so that everyone goes home having checked a to-do item off their list.

More tips on entertaining can be found in chapter 15.

From December 26 through mid-January, holiday items will be on sale. Stock up on wrapping paper, ribbons, cards, cookie tins, and the like so that you will already be ahead for next year.

part
three

the "get it
done!" system

how to do everything faster

(and better) and fit the things

you want into your life

13

"get it done!": the personal side

This chapter (and section) isn't about rushing. When I say that you'll get things done faster, I don't mean you'll have to move like a whirling dervish. This chapter is about establishing simple systems for all the things we have to do—and want to do—in daily life that simply take time.

When I visit clients, there are always some recurring themes to the conversation, and when it comes to getting things done, there are a few comments I hear from almost every client.

- "I just don't have time to get to the gym."
- "I don't have time to read anymore. I don't even get through the newspaper most mornings."
- "I rarely have time to see my friends—between working and the family, I'm just totally booked."
- "I don't have any hobbies—there's no time."

The systems explained in this chapter will help you change your habits. You *do* have the time, if you make any one of these items, or all of them, a priority.

The key lies in establishing simple systems for the items you need or want to make part of your life. We'll start out with some simple systems for some of the "would like to do" things because they aren't written about very often. The chapter will conclude with some systems and speed tips for the have-to-do tasks like getting dressed and shopping. By saving a few minutes on your morning routine, you will have a few extra minutes for reading the newspaper. Everything is ultimately interrelated. (There are more speed tips in chapters 14 and 15.)

finding time to exercise

Along with its physical benefits, exercise improves your mood and sense of well-being. But our lifestyles are very sedentary, and with so many conveniences in this day and age, everyone needs to concentrate on ways to keep moving. Here are some methods for slipping exercise into your week.

■ Use your lunch hour for exercise a couple of days per week. Some companies have on-site gyms for employees, but if a gym and a shower are not midday possibilities for you, then a good brisk walk is a great way to burn calories and to stay fit. You can supplement this routine with an upper body workout on the weekends.

■ Join a gym or commit to attending an exercise class with a friend—have a buddy system for making certain you get there regularly. It's more fun, too.

■ Get out and play with your kids. Take a walk, toss around a ball, take up a sport with them—tennis lessons for the family?

■ Walk your dog. If you develop a system of walking in the morning or when you get home from work, your four-legged friend won't let you forget that it's leash time.

■ Tone your muscles while you're doing other things.

Stand while you read the newspaper or open the mail. We sit all day, and the very act of standing up offers our muscles variety.

Stand up and exercise during commercials.

Do isometrics while waiting in line or when stopped at a red light.

finding time to stay on top of the news

Every day we are confronted with an overwhelming amount of information. To stay on top of what is happening in the world, here are some strategies.

- Pick a daily news source and stick with it. Most people don't need to follow three newspapers. The most important news will be covered no matter the paper you read. I do believe, however, that it's worth following a print newspaper. The front page of a print newspaper presents the top news stories we need to follow to be informed citizens.

- Skip some of the daily reports on issues like a pending report from Congress on Medicare. There will be a summation story later on that will put the daily dealings in perspective.

- Listen to news radio in the car or while doing chores.

- Weekly news magazines are repetitive if you are reading a regular newspaper, but they are excellent for their in-depth reports. So skip the news articles and go for the more extended coverage of the subjects that interest you.

---

sanity  saver

THE TEN-SECOND RULE
FOR FINISHING UP

Having numerous little chores left undone—drugstore purchases to put away, laundry to complete, counters to wipe, wastebaskets to empty, dry cleaning to sort, children's toys to put away—is one of the reasons we all feel so stressed for time. To keep your to-do list as short as possible, I recommend using the ten-second rule. If it takes only ten seconds to finish a job—putting the cap on the toothpaste, stowing the clean silverware back in the drawer, hanging up your coat—then do it right away. A moment spent now saves time later on.

■ Sign up for an online news-feed service, These RSS-feeds weed through and send you the best information on the subjects that interest you. (RSS stands for real simple syndication—a format for syndicating news and content.) You can sign up online or buy software that lets you follow both news and blogs on specific interests such as politics, the advertising industry, environmental news, finance, technology, or Hollywood gossip.

make time for reading

"I just don't have the time" is frequently the excuse used by someone who has failed to get through the latest novel he or she intended to read. But you *do* have the time, if you make reading a priority.

If you're really serious about finally getting back into the habit of reading—and it *is* a habit that becomes easier if you do it regularly—then go back to the system most of us used in school. Either set a specific amount of time to read each day, which can be as little as fifteen minutes, or set a specific number of pages. Your involvement in the book will grow as you make the commitment. Each day, your excitement about this new time you've given yourself will increase. In turn, this excitement will reinforce the habit.

Now that you've made the commitment to reading more, you need something to read. When selecting a book, you can suit your mood. Decide whether you want the fun of a mystery, the challenge of a more literary work, or the education offered in a nonfiction book. Now it's time to dive into that book. Good readers say they give every book a fair chance, but they don't force themselves to finish a book. There are too many great books to read. Reading shouldn't feel like work.

To help you make more time for reading, take reading material with you everywhere. You can get a lot of pages in while waiting at the dentist's or sitting in the car waiting until your child finishes hockey practice. If you're going out for the day, use a tote bag to take along reading for the train or if you have to wait for an appointment. One client refuses to buy a pocketbook unless it's large enough to hold a paperback book or a magazine, and she never leaves home without something to read. "If I'm meeting a friend for lunch, I don't mind waiting five to ten minutes if I have something to read," she says.

As you read more and more each day, you'll begin to explore different sources of reading materials. Use your library. Most libraries permit you to reserve and renew books online. Borrowing books takes the sting out of buying them, and the deadline of finishing before the due date provides a goal. Also, consider audiobooks—you can buy them, borrow them from the library, or download digital book files to your MP3 player. By being able to listen to books in the car or anyplace else, you will greatly expand the amount of time you can devote to reading.

It is also helpful to keep current reading materials in the room where they're likely to be read, neatly stored in baskets or containers.

Many people read more than one book at a time. They like the variety of having different books to suit their current mood. If you want to do the same, be sure one is a paperback so that you have one book that is portable.

Faster Reading for Business

- If your reading material requires you to concentrate, go to a separate room or wait for a quiet time so that you can read without distraction.

- Scan the table of contents of the book or the magazine.

- Skim each section in advance to determine what topics are important. Subheads and headlines will tip you off as to what is worth reading.

- Read the paragraphs at the end of each important chapter first. These paragraphs are often a condensed version of the chapter's most important information.

- Use a highlighter to mark the most important information.

- With magazines, set a time limit for a publication. For example, if a magazine comes weekly, you probably only want to spend forty-five minutes or so reading it. Keep that in mind as you go through the publication—yes, that amazing but lengthy article about the serial murderer looks pretty interesting, but do you really want to spend the extra time it will take to read all eight magazine pages of the story? You need to be selective in your reading so that this issue will be on its way out of the house before the next one comes in. With monthly publications, of course, you can afford to devote a little more time to each issue.

- Tear out articles so that you can take them with you to read.

■ To avoid accumulating newspapers and magazines, read and then recycle—or pass on to a friend.

finding time for friends

Family and friends are our most important commodities, and most of us are good at staying in touch with a core group of people. For those you would like to have more time for, here are some suggestions.

■ Create an exercise schedule where you walk with different people on different days.

■ Create a book club with a broad assortment of your friends.

■ Establish e-mail contact with old friends who now live far away.

■ When traveling for business, plan ahead and set up a dinner with friends in the city you're visiting. We're all so much more mobile now that it's generally easy to find an old acquaintance anywhere you go!

making time for hobbies

Schedule in time for your hobby. Whether it's thirty minutes each evening or two hours on the weekend, if it's important to you, then you owe it to yourself to make time for it.

If you can, dedicate space for your hobby. Both a woodworker and a quilter will find it much easier to work for just a few minutes if they have

sanity saver

CAPTURING YOUR IDEAS

How often have you had a great idea while driving, while waiting at an appointment, when having lunch with someone, only to forget what it was by later in the day?

Put pen and paper in the car and in every room for noting down ideas. In the car, you may find a small tape recorder to be handy for capturing great ideas.

space to organize their supplies and a permanently dedicated table for projects. One section of a finished basement or even a corner of a family room could become an appropriate work space for you. If your hobby has supplies, visit a store that specializes in containers, and purchase a drawer set or a couple of plastic boxes that will help you to store everything together.

faster dressing

We all have to get dressed in the morning. It is a relatively simple process if we open our sock drawer and can easily find matching socks, if the jacket hem that needed a few stitches has been mended and the jacket hung up, and if the shirt or blouse we plan to wear is clean and pressed. If these things aren't taken care of, or if the closet floor is strewn with clothing and shoes, then a simple act like getting dressed can be a nightmare. (If you have kids, that nightmare is multiplied.)

- Sort through your closet and save only the items that you enjoy wearing. A basic business wardrobe should consist of only fifteen pieces. These can be assembled and reassembled into thirty to forty different outfits, which are enough changes for two months' worth of workdays.

- If you have trouble pulling outfits together in the mornings, take snapshots of your outfits as they should be accessorized. These photos will be quick reminders for you.

- Build your wardrobe around one or two main colors to make it easier to match accessories. A basic color scheme will also minimize the number of choices you need for shoe colors, and so forth.

- If you wear a lot of black or navy, commit to one color or the other. They wear similarly, and by choosing one, it will be easier to organize your closet and to match accessories. I met a friend just the other day who was wearing a stunning black jacket. The only problem was she had gotten dressed in the dimness of early morning, and by midday light it was very clear that her pants were most definitely navy.

- Don't buy high-maintenance clothes. For example, linen wrinkles easily and requires frequent pressing.

- Invest in a ready-to-go year-round dress in a dark or neutral color. You can dress it up or down with jackets, scarves, or belts.

- Hang your clothes in categories so you can find what you want quickly.

- If you have similar items, such as several pairs of black pants or navy skirts, write a short description of the item, such as "black pants" or "flare leg," on an index card, punch a hole in the corner, and use some yarn to tie the label onto the hanger. The extra moments this takes now will save you time on mornings when you're trying to rush out of the house. When your clothing comes back from the cleaners, be sure to sort it out onto the appropriately labeled hanger.

- If you have the space, store summer and winter clothing in separate closets. Your closet will be more convenient to use if it's holding only the current season's clothes.

- Update your accessories regularly. By accessorizing with today's fashion add-ons, most people can maintain a basic wardrobe of items they like without having to update as frequently.

- Get rid of clothes you don't wear. A stuffed closet takes time to manage.

- If a suit is only lightly wrinkled, try hanging it in the bathroom while you're showering so that the steam smoothes out the wrinkles.

time booster

QUICK-CHANGE ARTIST

Going out after work? Wear a simple suit to work. Take off the jacket and switch to a more fun top for the evening.

organize your handbag

To organize for life on the run, you need a handbag where you can stash neatly and securely the things you must carry with you.

- Choose a bag with pockets and a zipper compartment, and be sure that it's designed in a style that will close securely.

- Be sure there is a safe but accessible pocket for your keys.

- For easy cash management, organize the money in your wallet by denomination, small bills first.

- Only carry the credit cards you use regularly. Make a copy of their numbers for safekeeping at home.

- Always have a pen and paper or a small notebook.

- Store your business cards in a small card case to keep them from getting shopworn.

- Create a small emergency kit for your bag. Use a three-by-five-inch cosmetics bag to carry a first-aid kit, hair tiebacks, safety pins, spare house and car keys, aspirin, nail file, mini tape measure, and a list of emergency phone numbers.

- Purchase a small pouch to use as a cosmetics bag, or as a small purse to take with you at lunch instead of carrying a full handbag.

grooming

Statistics show that the typical American male spends twenty-three minutes each day on grooming. That is less than half an hour for showering, shampooing, skin care, and shaving. Most women find their routine takes longer than that. But even men can knock time off their routine by doubling up on products. For example, they can use an aftershave splash that doubles as a moisturizer. Following are ways to make your grooming routine more efficient.

---

time ⏱ booster

EASIER HANDBAG MANAGEMENT

Don't switch handbags, or you are likely to leave something behind. Pick one purse and use it for every occasion except more formal ones. For those events, pack only the essentials such as money, keys, lip balm, and so on.

- Speed up your ability to get ready for the day quickly by placing all hair, skin, and cosmetic supplies in an accessible place so that you have everything within easy reach.

- Purchase a clock for the bathroom. Then calculate how long you spend on your hair and makeup. Each day stick to the same amount of time.

- Consider whether a simpler hairstyle might be worth the time savings.

- Purge the old. Get rid of products you haven't used in a year.

- Visit a makeup counter at a department store and ask for up-to-date time-saving ideas for your morning routine. New products and new systems will save you time and update your look, which are both worthy goals.

- Look for multipurpose beauty products such as a two-in-one shampoo and conditioner. If you use hair gel, switch to a spritz style that serves as both a gel and a spray.

- Try shower shortcuts. After you put conditioner on your hair, comb it out so you won't have to detangle later.

- Shaving while in the shower will help this task go more quickly and be easier on the skin.

- Opt for leg waxing. It lasts about six weeks and you'll save time by not shaving.

- Make makeup last. Choose long-wearing cosmetics, smudge-proof lipstick and foundation, and waterproof mascara.

- Use foundation with sunscreen—one product instead of two.

- Don't have time to put on foundation? Use a quick brush of bronzing powder instead.

- For a fast base, apply concealer in a shade one tone lighter than your natural skin color under your eyes and over any blemishes. Then powder and go.

These manicure tips will keep your nails looking great seven days a week.

- Pick sheer, pale colors. They show chips less than deeper tones and require less maintenance.

- Go bright for a weekend party by putting a new color over your pale base.

- Try one-coat, long-wearing and two-in-one basecoat/top coat polishes.

- Apply polish in thin coats and they'll dry faster, particularly if you put your finished nails into a basin of water filled with ice cubes.

shopping secrets that save time

Sometimes shopping is a pleasurable way to spend time. Other times, you just have errands to run quickly.

for women

- Take inventory of what you already own before you shop for something new.

- Shop with a well-thought-out to-do list. Plan your route through the mall (or through town) based on convenience. If the trip is for items to wear, visit the shoe store last. Shoe purchases are heavy and bulky to carry around, and you'll make better shoe choices if you know what clothing you've purchased.

- Wear easy-to-put-on clothing to save time in the dressing room but dress neatly. If you look sloppy, you're not going to be treated as seriously by the salespeople. Slip-on shoes are a must for easy clothing changes. They will simplify your life if you need to run back out to the display floor to grab a different size.

- Go early. You're fresher—and so are the employees—and stores won't be as crowded.

- Shop during off-peak hours. Parking is easier, there are fewer lines, and the salespeople are in better spirits and can help you. Also, try to shop during the middle of the week when new merchandise is more likely to be out.

- Understanding a store layout can often aid in shopping efficiently. In general, stores put the trendier items toward the front, so if you're looking for the latest fashion, poke around in the front of the store. Basic items are usually displayed in the middle of the store; sale items are located toward the back.

■ If your goal is a quick shopping trip, go alone. Although shopping with a friend is more fun, studies show that when people shop together they make it more of an event, and as a result, it takes longer.

■ For just a couple of items, you may do better at a boutique than at the mall.

■ Limit yourself to two department stores. Most carry the popular brands from the specialty stores, and by limiting yourself to a few stores, you can get to know the merchandise, follow the ads, and make a point of shopping on sale days. You may also benefit from one or both of the store's reward or points programs.

■ Seek out effective salespeople. A good one (particularly one on commission) may actually phone you when the store receives something that you are looking for or that she or he thinks you might like.

■ Buy it when you see it. How many times have you found the perfect gift or the perfect dress and waited, only to decide that it really was just what you wanted and by time you went back for it, it was sold out? Not quite sure you want the item? If you've found something and you *think* it's right, buy it anyway. You can always return it. If you wait, you may find it's difficult to find the style or color or size you are looking for. (Note that brick-and-mortar stores may still be selling an item that is no longer available online.)

■ If you buy a skirt, buy a blouse to go with it. Looking for the right match weeks later will just waste your time.

■ Pick up needed accessories at the time you shop for outfits.

■ If you travel for business, make practical selections; pick clothes that are easy to care for.

■ If there is a long line at the cash register, ask about your options: Can you pay in another department? Can you put the item on hold and buy it at a less busy time? Can you order it online? Can the clerk hold it for you and ring it up later, and you'll stop back to pick it up before leaving?

for men

- Select a store that sells the style of suits or clothing you like. Assess the salespeople. If you find one who seems sharp, request that he or she call you when the store is having a sale or when new merchandise he or she thinks you'd like comes in.

- Stay with one family of colors. If you wear lots of navy and gray, don't add a brown suit. Too many color options make both shopping and travel more complicated, as different shoes, shirts, and ties may be needed to coordinate outfits.

- Order sports shirts on the Internet. Sizes of shirts don't vary too much, and with a couple of clicks of the mouse you'll be able to refresh your weekend wardrobe.

- Let others shop for you. Provide relatives or your significant other with an index card with your various sizes. On special occasions you'll receive a shirt or a tie or a sweater or socks you can use instead of getting another useless paperweight or travel flashlight—and better yet, you didn't have to spend time shopping!

14

"get it done!"
at home

Shortcuts and speed tips are absolutely necessary at home because we all have so many chores to do. From quick and efficient ways to get regular errands done to finding ways to locate customer service when your brand-new dryer conks out or the guaranteed delivery of flowers to your mother-in-law on her birthday is late, this chapter will help you navigate these daily details with ease to create more time for yourself.

When I visit homes on consultations, people complain about all the errands on their to-do lists and how much of their personal time these chores consume. (Those with young children find errands particularly challenging as they often have to allot double the time when they have little ones in tow.) Yet errands can be handled quickly and efficiently—if you're organized.

One of my clients just never could manage to plan ahead. She would get up on Saturdays to find her day off consisting of continual in-and-out errands. "I would get home from the grocery store and realize I forgot to pick up my shoes from the shoemaker," she explained. "Later my kids would need a ride somewhere. I would drop them off and then I'd make another stop or two on the way home. Then they would call to be picked up, and they would need some type of school supply so we would stop at yet another store. I don't think I ever had more than about twenty minutes at home to get anything done."

After consulting me, this single mother implemented a household errands list and taught her family to add to it—as well as write down items on the grocery list (see chapter 9)—so that she could run errands in a more orderly fashion. Sarah was the first to admit that she was her own worst enemy when it came to errand organization, but her frustration at having no weekend time was very motivating, and she soon led her family to reform.

From completing errands to avoiding losing track of items to enlisting a customer service person's help, great ways to get things done are covered in the next few sections.

errands

Everyone has to do errands, and the worst part is that they repeat every week—sometimes twice a week, between picking up milk, getting bananas, refilling prescriptions, and dropping off the dry cleaning. Here are some ways to get your errands done more efficiently.

- *Keep a running list.* Ask all family members to take responsibility for writing things down on the list. From "buy stapler" to "return library books," the tasks should be written down.

- *When you can, use the phone, not the car.* If you're looking for a particular item, call ahead and ask if a store has it. Then ask the clerk to hold it for you for a particular amount of time.

- *Go online.* From pharmacy items and specialty teas to holiday gifts, you can order a great deal through the Internet. If you establish an account with a company, an order can be placed with only a couple of clicks.

- *Use stores with drive-through convenience windows, such as banks and pharmacies.* You needn't spend time or money on parking—you don't even have to get out of your car.

- *Make a list of all your intended stops for the day and then plan your route at breakfast time.* By planning well geographically, you can save time.

- *Group your errands.* By working with an errands list and devoting a couple of hours once or twice a week to doing them, you ought to be able to keep your errands from eating up all your time.

- *Try to get your errands done at nonrush times.* Some people like to run a couple of errands on their way to work (drop off dry cleaning, stop at pharmacy) when the establishments aren't crowded and it's possible to get in and out quickly. Use time-saving delivery services when possible.

- *Ask for help from your family.* Your spouse and any teenagers are all capable of getting things done. If you prefer, you can make it a family activity. At a shopping center, let everyone fan out in different directions, and meet back at the car.

- *Weigh time savings against dollar savings.* The family brand of toothpaste may be going on sale at the drugstore the next day, but if you're at the grocery store—and have no other pharmacy errands that week—it may make more sense to just buy the toothpaste with the groceries.

---

sanity  saver

MINIMIZING HASSLES BY AVOIDING CLUTTER ("FREE" STUFF COMES WITH A PRICE)

Stop! Don't buy—or take—something just because it's cheap or free. If you don't really need or want an item, don't bring it home.

The sale on a new scent at the drugstore, the take-home favor from the bridal shower, the freebie items when you purchase new cosmetics, the paperback books your coworker is offering you— don't take these things unless you see an immediate use for them. Or if they do follow you home, such as with the sample makeup products the cosmetic companies give out, share them with others or dispose of them right away. Don't let them become clutter in your house.

■ *When you come home, put everything away soon after arrival.* Enlist help from family members even if they didn't go shopping with you. If you leave the purchases here "for now," you'll find that they'll likely sit there too long.

"do it yourself" is not always necessary

Some shortcuts actually work better if you join forces with other like-minded people. Start a neighborhood errand cooperative. One person watches the kids while one or two others run everyone's errands. The following week you switch jobs.

If a neighborhood cooperative isn't practical for you, consider using errand services. In big cities, some apartment buildings have concierge services, while major office buildings sometimes have errand-running services available (for a fee) to workers in the building. You phone in for anything from picking up dry cleaning to standing in line at the DMV for license plate exchanges to dropping off your car to be serviced. If you aren't in a major metropolitan area, you may still find that new businesses have popped up to fill consumers' changing needs. There are rent-a-wife services—rent-a-hubby services are also popular, but they tend to specialize in repairs—in some areas, and businesses like driving schools may also offer DMV-related errand-type services. Even some child care centers offer everything from extended hours or enrichment classes to haircuts and dry cleaning drop-off.

lost items

Losing things—such as keys, tickets, your glasses, or the invitation with the address you need—wastes a lot of time. Any system you can establish that helps you keep track of your things is well worth your time. These six steps will get you started.

1. *Create a sense of order.* Establish a bowl for keys, a drawer for tickets, a file for upcoming events and related information. Put your keys and glasses in the same place all the time so that you won't lose them. Teach family members to respect this system.

2. *Store things near where they are used.* For example, the key to the cabinet in the basement should be stored near the basement stairs.

3. *Train family members to be responsible for their own stuff—and to put back anything of yours that they use.*

4. *Pay attention to what you're doing.* Always be alert. Whether parking your car or taking off your glasses, note your surroundings.

---

quick **GO!** start

TAKE ADVANTAGE OF RANDOM BENEFITS

If you work for a major company, keep your ears open for unusual benefits. From flu shots to income tax preparation advice, some companies arrange for special opportunities for employees, and you may want to take advantage of them.

---

5. *Create images to help you remember.* If you parked your car in the B8 section of the garage, think of your eighth birthday as you leave the garage. Not only will this help you remember B8, but the memories will likely make you smile.

6. *Stress often makes you forgetful.* Reduce stress through learning some relaxation techniques. An easy one is simply focusing on breathing deeply and evenly. By gaining control of your breath and ensuring that you're taking in enough oxygen, you'll soon find yourself feeling less stressed.

labeling

If your belongings are labeled, they'll be easier to identify if they go astray or are borrowed by others.

- Label your garbage cans and lids with dark markers. Your address is more helpful than a name.

- Label wooden tools with a permanent marker so that you can loan them occasionally but still get them back.

- Books are always being borrowed—and are rarely returned. Are you good at calligraphy or do you have great handwriting? Then write your name in yourself. Or use bookplates from stationery and bookstores, or purchase an embosser from a specialty store.

ONE DAY, NO CAR KEYS TO LOSE?

Keyless cars are on their way. Instead of running on a mechanical key, these cars start based on the readout of a credit-card-size system that you carry in your wallet. When you are within about ten feet of the car, the system unlocks your car and a button in the car lets you start or stop the engine—but only if the card is inside the car, too.

- Serving dishes that you sometimes take to the neighborhood potluck dinner can be labeled using a permanent marker. The ink won't cook off or wash away. (Or buy some of the inexpensive colorful plastic dishes and serving bowls at garage sales and don't worry about collecting them to bring home.)
- Label DVDs and CDs with permanent markers. Mark on the matte side, not the bottom playing side.
- Clothes can be marked with laundry pens, iron-on labels, and cloth name tags. To stand up to a summer's worth of camp laundry, sewn-in tags work best.
- To identify luggage or backpacks, use colorful labels that help yours stand out at the airport. For suitcases, put on a cell phone number, not your home address. You don't want to signal to someone that your house is unattended.
- No one wants to mix up their wineglasses at a dinner party, so consider wine charms. Paper wine tags that label glasses in the same way but are less costly for the host to provide are also available.
- For both cell phones and sports equipment, get deface-proof labels that won't wear off or tear off.

here's what to do before you lose your . . .

In spite of our best precautions, sometimes we will lose valuable items through accident or theft. Here are steps to take in advance that will help you in the event of a loss.

Wallet

- Photocopy your wallet's contents, including the front and back of the following: driver's license, health insurance cards, credit and debit cards, and other cards (gym membership card, for instance). This will give you the pertinent information as well as the customer service number of each item. Make two copies and store one at home and one at work.

- Don't carry your Social Security card in your wallet. You rarely need it, and identity theft is all too easy if it falls into the wrong hands.

- Separate your bank accounts. Make sure your debit card doesn't give access to all your bank accounts.

Cell Phone

- Store a list of the numbers you enter in your cell phone address book elsewhere.

- If you lose your phone, call it. There is a chance that the person who finds the phone will return it if he or she knows how to find you.

sanity saver

STOLEN WALLET

If your wallet is stolen, call the local police precinct and file a report. Give the report number to your bank and your credit-card companies when you report the loss of any banking-related information or your credit cards. Contact all three major credit bureaus (Equifax, 800-685-1111; Experian, 888-397-3742; Trans Union, 800-916-8800) and explain what happened. They will file a fraud alert and send you a free credit report to monitor suspicious activity.

Consider a for-fee company that takes charge of canceling all the necessary credit and debit cards in case of theft or loss. For example, for an annual fee, one major credit-card company will cancel all your cards for you and put a fraud alert on your accounts. In some states, the company can replace your driver's license and passport as well.

Keys

- Don't label your keys.
- Leave a spare set with a trusted friend.
- Don't carry safe deposit keys—ever.
- Don't attach key-chain membership cards. If your gym or video store has lax security, someone who finds your keys might be able to access your personal information.

Personal Organizer/Calendar

- Label your organizer clearly with your name and cell phone number.
- Remove passed months from paper calendars so that you don't risk losing miscellaneous but valuable papers.
- Create a backup file by photocopying addresses, phone numbers, and other important information.

Personal Digital Assistants

- Back up regularly.
- Create a password so others can't access your PDA.

Laptop

- Back up your hard drive regularly.
- Laptops are valuable, so don't leave yours unattended.
- Record the serial and model numbers and establish a password.
- Your laptop should always be with you. Don't put it in a checked bag when traveling.

Pet

- Every pet should have a collar and a tag with your phone number.
- Collar tags can get lost or torn off, so also ask your vet about the new computer chips that are being implanted in some animals. A onetime insertion of the chip by the veterinarian will provide a method for an animal shelter to identify the pet and get in touch with you if your animal is ever lost or stolen.

thinking of others: cards and gifts made simple

Although it's always supposed to be the thought that counts, somehow it never feels that way when you suddenly realize that you have to make time to pick up a get-well card, a belated birthday card, or a hostess gift for the dinner party you're attending. You can save yourself time and stress with the following tips.

- Stock up on greeting cards, from condolence and get-well cards to birthday cards for friends and relatives. When you suddenly realize you have to send a card, you need go no farther than your desk drawer or cabinet. Another benefit to this system is that it's actually fun to shop for cards if you have the time to spend. You now have something fun to do while another family member finishes cruising the aisles at the drugstore, or you can shop for cards at an airport gift shop while waiting for a connecting flight.

- Always keep a good supply of stamps around. Order online or from 1-800-STAMPS24.

- Use online cards. A site you use regularly will also generally e-mail you date reminders.

- Purchase a variety of gifts to have on hand. Although you will want to shop for that special gift for your sister or best friend, it's awfully nice to be able to reach into the closet and pull out a token gift for an office birthday or a hostess gift. If you set about to select a variety of items, you'll find it's easy. In the meantime, consider picking up items along the following lines: guest soaps, bookplates, striped socks, novelty pens, portable photo albums, flavored teas or coffees, or travel essentials. For children or for baby gifts, think about having on hand baby or children's books, board games, or coloring books.

- For the more personal gifts you want to purchase for friends and family, create a gift file and make notes on sizes, color preferences, and other details. Also keep a running record of what you've given them. You don't really want to give your dad a golf sweater three years in a row, even if he does like to golf.

■ Make gift buying a year-round process. You'll not only save time but you might also save money if you find a great gift item on sale. Ideally, the proper place to store these gifts is a designated shelf in a linen closet or an extra cupboard, but if a particular gift is an awkward size, be sure to write yourself a note that not only reminds you that you have it but tells you where it's stored.

customer service

Customer service is becoming a thing of the past. Companies think that because you can find out about so many things on their Web site, they have less obligation to staff their companies with live people to help you. Yet, almost every week something comes up and we need to phone a company for information, for a question regarding a bill, for directions on sending something back to the company—the list goes on. But when you try to contact the company, of course, you end up in an automated circle that you can't break out of.

how to reach a customer service rep on the phone

Today's phone systems often feature "prompt menus" that require you to push numbers according to the company plan to get anywhere near a person who might help you out. Even if you were in a good mood when you first placed the phone call, it's difficult to keep smiling by the time you go through several prompts—only to be told that "all customer service representatives are busy," with a recommendation that you visit the company's Web site instead.

Here are some secret methods that will sometimes connect you to an actual human being.

■ Try working with the menu options. Some companies have created speedier systems, and they will tell you how to get directly to the proper party.

■ If the menu of options is excessive, try hitting "0" or "00." If it's a voice-recognition system, say "agent" or "representative" or "operator."

- If you call a particular company regularly, ask about its system and the proper number of the department that can help you. Then, note in your contact information what direct number to dial.

- Don't punch numbers in haste. If your finger hits a button in error, you may have to start the entire process again.

- Visit www.gethuman.com for the latest information on reaching a phone support person if entering "0" or "00" doesn't work.

how to get what you need from customer service without wasting too much time

Problems cost us time. Whether your refrigerator is on the fritz or your new sofa was delivered damaged or you are unhappy with the service you received at a restaurant, you want to believe there is a way to rectify the problem. The secret is to create an atmosphere that makes the customer service representative (or the management person assigned to deal with these issues) want to help you. Here are some tips for getting the help you want.

- Don't call when you're enraged. Tempting as it might be to want to blow off steam, the problem was not caused by the person you've phoned. All you will do if you yell at the representative is annoy him or her. Instead, your goal is to make the person *want* to help you.

- Explain the situation clearly and the action that needs to be taken, but do not blame the representative. For example, you might say, I know this isn't your fault, but my bank account isn't reflecting a deposit I made last week, and we need to find a way to resolve this."

- Call on Sunday mornings (if the company's customer service department is open) or during major sporting events, when fewer people call, so you can avoid a long wait on hold.

- Customer service people are sometimes rewarded for the speed at which they are able to clear up a problem. If you offer some suggestions on how your situation can be resolved, they may be more agreeable than you would expect.

■ At the beginning of the call, ask the agent's name. It personalizes the conversation. While agents have "heard everything" and aren't paid for being sympathetic, they are human and it may warm the conversation if you are able to call them by name. Later on, if you aren't satisfied, you can continue your discussion with a supervisor, and you will be able to identify who told you what as you worked your way through the system.

■ Conclude by asking the agent to summarize what was accomplished and what will happen next.

15

"get it done!" while commuting, traveling, just having fun, or sleeping

*f*rom commuting and traveling to entertaining and trying to get a good night's sleep, it's all in the approach. These aspects of life can be drudgery—one more hassle to tolerate—or they can be a smooth-running part of our lives that let us actually enjoy ourselves in the process.

home away from home: your car

Our cars have almost become mini-mobile homes. Unfortunately, there is not always any emphasis on order—or cleanliness. When I lived in the city and would take a train out to visit clients, they would pick me up at the train station, and only after I opened the passenger door would they try to address the fact that there really was no room for me. I've had clients remove piles of papers for the office and wipe off the seat the remains of their child's peanut-butter sandwich; dry cleaning and errand-related items were almost always spread out in both the front seats and backseats. While the advantage of a car over public transportation is that you can use it to store certain items before you have time to take care of them, it's important to be tidy about it. An organized car—just like an organized household—makes it easier for you to function seamlessly. You won't waste time looking for lost items under the seats because this space will be organized.

- Buy a visor organizer (available in auto-supply stores). Use it to store extra change for tolls or your state's speedy pass for going through tolls, gas and toll receipts, and a small pen and pad of paper.

- Look for front-seat and backseat organizers and some type of trash system that will work in your car. Keep a bin or a collapsible crate in the trunk of the car to prevent groceries and other purchases from rolling around. It also facilitates bringing packages in from the car—just pick up the crate and carry it in.

- Use organizers for businesspeople; some provide space for files, laptop, tape measure, ruler, and so on for a truly on-the-road office.

- Clean out your glove compartment! It should only include automobile information, such as the car's registration papers and auto insurance card, and other important items, such as emergency telephone numbers, emergency money, and a flashlight.

- Buy for your vehicle a roll of paper towels, a box of wipes, tissues, extra garbage bags, an umbrella, and nonperishable snacks, which could come in handy—particularly if you have children. Store these items in a box or a container that is out of the way but still accessible.

Avoid a car key hunt by having a specific place where you always put your keys. Also, establish a spot for keeping copies of keys for all cars that you drive in case you unexpectedly need to use a different car. Color coding the key ring according to the color of the car will help you identify different car keys quickly.

Start a file for car maintenance records with your other home files or keep a running log in the glove compartment.

navigating while on the go

Now that your vehicle is clean, organized, and stocked for any emergency, do you know how to get to where you are going?

- If you have the option of getting a GPS system in your next car, it's worth the investment. The system will help you avoid getting lost by keeping you oriented, which will save you time on the road.

- Print out directions from the Internet. Although this information is usually helpful, the systems are not yet perfect, and you may still need a map to figure out certain details of the trip.

- Always have an area map in the car. No matter how terrific the GPS system or how detailed the directions you printed out from the Internet, when you are totally lost a map will help.

commuting

Almost everyone who works must factor commuting time into their day. A study undertaken by the Texas Transportation Institute in its annual report on congestion in urban areas found that Americans spend triple the amount of time in traffic than they did twenty years ago. Another study from California revealed that drivers in Los Angeles spend an average of fifty-six hours per year—more than a full workweek—stuck in traffic. In Atlanta, the figure is fifty-three hours. We can rarely use a beat-the-rush-hour-traffic strategy anymore because rush hour now extends for about three hours during the mornings and another three hours during the evening drive time.

Although some self-employed people and telecommuters need only worry about getting to another part of their house, most of us must find ways to make commuting as tolerable as possible—without switching jobs.

- Use public transportation if possible. If you live in a part of the country where there is bus, train, or subway service, mass transit simplifies your life by freeing up your commuting hours for doing small tasks—or for time for you. You can spend the time reading, catching up on e-mail (for those with wireless handheld devices), list making, or writing business memos. (Using public transportation time to catch up with making phone calls should be done sparingly as it is often bothersome to those around you.)

- If you ride the bus or the subway, you can sometimes get off a few stops early to run some errands or to enjoy a brisk walk.

- Combine commuting with exercise. Can you walk or bike to work?

- Ask whether you can telecommute one day each week. Although most jobs still require on-scene presence much of the time, one day per week working from home can make you a more productive worker—providing you with uninterrupted work time with no one to bother you.

- If you drive, you still have ways to take control. Begin by considering both your travel start time and your route—you may be able to save time on the road by leaving home thirty minutes earlier to drive during a less busy time. (Perhaps you'll be able to leave work a little earlier or take a longer lunch to run errands to regain some personal time.)

- Listen to educational CDs or audiobooks in the car. They're almost as good as gaining extra hours to read.

- Use drive time as "idea" time. Buy one of the autopads (with pen attached) for your car so that you can make quick notes while stopped at a light.

- Plan out your day while driving.

- If you drive to and from client offices for meetings or sales calls, consider tape-recording your thoughts as you drive and then playing them back later on. If you tape interviews while on a site visit, you can listen to them on the way home.

- If your company or town provides a commuter van, this is a good option because it frees you from driving yourself. Discuss ground rules with the other "regulars." Perhaps you can work or read the paper during morning drive time and catch up with others in the afternoons.

getting there with half the hassle: the best travel tips

Americans are taking shorter vacations but more of them. Some are as brief as one to two days; others more commonly are three to five. And a benefit to short trips is that they are easier to get ready for, which makes them easier to slot into our lives.

- Join hotel and airline frequent customer memberships and take advantage of benefits such as free flights, first-class upgrades, early check-ins, late checkouts, and room upgrades.

- Purchase a spare phone charger and keep it permanently packed so that there is one less thing to pack when you travel.

- In preparation for travel:

    Check with your insurance carrier or credit-card company to see if they provide coverage for overseas medical emergencies and evacuations.

    Discuss directly with your insurance provider health insurance procedures and medical challenges you may have before traveling outside your coverage area.

- Keep a permanent packing and pre-trip to-do list. Note on it everything from stopping the newspaper delivery to packing toothbrushes.

- Leave a copy of your itinerary at home and at work. Include transportation information, departure and arrival dates and times, flight numbers, addresses, and phone numbers for where you are staying.

- For a longer trip or a family vacation, start organizing to leave about a week ahead of time. Call to have the newspapers canceled for the specified dates, ask a neighbor to collect your mail and hold it for you (or have the post office hold it), and so forth.

- If you take an annual camping or ski vacation and don't use the equipment in between, empty the bag after the trip and then wash and repack, and you're all set for the following year. If you noticed anything you were missing this year, pin a note to the suitcase as a reminder to check sizes to or buy a replacement for something you lost along the way.

- Download movies to your PC. There are now an increasing number of sites that permit downloading legally. And you can still curl up on the couch at your destination to watch the movie—just put your laptop on a small table nearby.

- Lay your clothing out in advance so you can assess colors

and accessories. Don't take anything "just in case." If you really have an emergency, you can purchase something new at your destination. Think layers; it's the easiest way to prepare for unpredictable weather. Pack one pair of dress shoes and wear your walking shoes. Consider taking a travel-size umbrella and spot remover, and if you are going overseas, be sure to take an adapter.

- Store a box of plastic resealable bags in your closet or the room where you pack. Place all toiletries (and anything else you want to keep grouped together such as wires for your laptop) inside a plastic bag to make luggage inspection neater. This will also make it easier to reassemble your belongings if your bag must be opened and searched.

- Put items you don't want to forget in a specific place during the week so you will remember to pack them.

- Send bulky baggage and cumbersome items to your destination ahead of time. Ask the hotel staff or the lodging host for specific handling instructions and call ahead to check that your baggage has arrived.

- With the new airport security measures now in place, save travel time by packing lightly. Plan to wear your bulkiest outfit so that you don't need to try to pack it.

- With all the security changes for air travel, check www.tsa.gov for the latest in packing regulations. As of this writing, only small quantities of certain liquids are permitted on board—meaning that most liquid items such as toiletries have to be packed in checked bags. You can travel with these items—they just aren't permitted in the passenger cabin. If you feel strongly about keeping your toiletry bag with you, switch to powder and nonliquid substitutes for your personal care products; some travelers are shipping their toiletry bags by overnight express so that they don't need to worry about traveling with these items. Some hotels that cater to a business clientele are working out ways for frequent guests to stock a supply of toiletries at the hotel so that personal items are waiting for travelers when they return. These rules may change over time, so check the government Web site to see what is applicable for your next trip.

■ Purchase small travel containers and fill them with the products you use. Buy small labels or use file folder labels to note what is in each one.

■ Select multitasking products if you can. Pack an all-in-one shampoo/conditioner to reduce what you have to with you.

■ Put makeup brushes in an eyeglass case for safekeeping.

■ Pack an extra pair of prescription eyeglasses.

■ Pack a mini-flashlight in case of an emergency.

■ Take along a plastic bag for damp things such as swimsuits.

■ Travel stores now sell packing gear that squeezes the air out of clothing so that you can pack more in less space, but remember that everything weighs the same. Even if you have room for them, extra items may weigh more than you want to carry.

■ Put your identification inside your bag rather than outside of it.

■ For adventure trips, investigate clothing made of Gore-Tex and polypropylene fabrics, which are lightweight and dry very fast.

■ With children, be sure you have snacks in their carry-on bag as well as activities to keep them busy while traveling.

■ If you're vacationing and want to have space to bring home purchases, travel with an extra small soft-sided bag that can be packed in your regular bag until you are ready to fill it for your return trip home.

■ Use the plastic bags provided in your hotel room to store dirty laundry.

■ Airline food has always been terrible, so let the scarcity of meal service on shorter flights give you the impetus to do yourself a favor: bring your own food. Don't wait until the last minute when your only option is the pizza place across from the check-in gate. Pack a tasty lunch from home or run by your favorite deli before heading to the airport. (Call in advance and ask them to have it ready for you.) By planning ahead, you can eat more healthy fare, getting your trip off to a better start.

- If you're checking your luggage:

    Prepare a backpack or a carry-on bag with the basics you would need if your luggage doesn't reach your destination: medicine, allowed toiletries, jewelry and valuables, change of clothing, and underwear.

    Distribute belongings among the different suitcases of members of the family. That way if one bag goes astray, no one person has lost everything.

    Create a way for your luggage to be identified easily. Buy a brightly colored bag or tie a ribbon or some type of cloth on the handle. That way you won't lose the bag to someone grabbing it by mistake.

- Engage the auto reply function on your e-mail accounts and change your voice-mail messages. Be sure to change them back when you return.

- In the past, getting stuck in an airport relegated you to sitting in uncomfortable chairs and eating bad food, but now airports have totally changed. They can even be fun! Many offer various personal services ranging from massages and manicures to haircuts; others have gourmet restaurants and performances or art shows on loan from city museums. Airline clubs (at bigger airports) generally have a per-day fee for nonmembers. For fifty dollars or so you can have access to a shower as well as more comfortable seating and meeting and office facilities.

- Car rental firms are now renting out fast-pass transponders so that even people driving rental cars aren't stuck waiting in the cash line to pay tolls.

- Staying in a major convention hotel? To shorten what can be interminable waits for the elevator, book a room on a low floor. During high-traffic times, elevators stop more frequently on lower floors, so you'll get to your meetings more promptly.

entertaining

Who has time to entertain? You do. Here are some ways to have fun with friends with less work.

- Throw a potluck. Divvy up who brings what so that the prep work is evenly shared.

- If you hate to cook, buy. The big-box stores and an increasing number of grocery stores are beginning to carry appetizers in bulk at reasonable prices.

- Cook ahead—way ahead. Think through some of the dishes you'll want in December, and cook and freeze in November.

- Splurge on hiring someone to help out. Whether it's to tend the bar or clean up the kitchen, a paid pair of extra hands can make a big difference in your enjoyment.

- Have two or more events back-to-back. Once you're prepared for one, you might as well keep going. You might also consider a brunch instead of a dinner; it's generally an easier meal to make.

- Have one big bash instead of small parties.

Once your guests have been invited, take care of the following tasks.

- Evaluate your supplies—do you have enough plates? Napkins? Silver? If not, decide whether to buy or rent, or to use paper or plastic.

- Divide and conquer. Make two lists: a do-ahead list (buy paper goods, nonperishables, and other similar items.) and a last-minute list (time table, cooking chores, final house straightening, and so forth). Give yourself deadlines and delegate chores to others.

- When preparing hors d'oeuvres, consider preparing double and freezing one of the trays for another night.

- Keep a to-do list in the kitchen during any party. That way when you are refilling the hors d'oeuvres plate and talking to someone, you can still grab a quick look at what else needs to be done.

- Start a party file. Maintain an invitation list, menus, and post-party notes on what you would change for next time.

how to get a good night's sleep

In our time-pressured world, getting the sleep we need becomes harder and harder. We're wound up when we go to bed, so sleep comes slowly. When the alarm goes off in the morning, we're not fully rested. Unfortunately, poor sleep management affects our ability to enjoy the rest of the day. Here are some ways better organization can help you to get a better night's sleep.

- Know how much sleep you need. Start sleeping seven hours per night and see how you feel. After a week, if you find yourself waking up earlier than that, sleep fifteen minutes less for a full week; again, consider how you feel. If you feel like you still need more sleep than seven hours, start working toward going to bed a little earlier.

- Establish a regular bedtime and rising time. Rituals are beneficial.

- If you're a catnapper, try to nap before 3 P.M. Later naps can affect your ability to go to sleep at night.

- Check the medications you take. Dozens of widely used over-the-counter and prescription medicines contain caffeine and other ingredients that aren't conducive to sleep.

- If noise is the problem where you live:

    Consider a white noise machine to block out other sounds. You can set it for ocean, rain, crickets, a gentle wind, or many other soothing sounds. (You may derive the same benefit from turning on a fan or an air conditioner.)

    Some people listen to music or talk radio (if it doesn't bother other people) and find it helps them go to sleep.

    Try ear plugs. Drugstores sell packs of ten pairs for only a few dollars.

- If light is a problem, install blackout shades and turn your clock at an angle so that the display doesn't bother you.

- Good sleep hygiene consists of behaviors that are conducive to getting sleepy. Don't exercise or check e-mail right before bed, avoid caffeine from late afternoon on, and don't have a big meal too close to bedtime. Watching television or reading by a bright light can also be stimulating. Smaller book lights create a more peaceful environment. Soft music, soothing scents, and a cool room (about sixty-five degrees) help prepare you for drifting off to sleep.

relaxing at home

Rather than going through the effort and expense of escaping for a few days, consider what many people think of as the perfect vacation: staying home. The trick is to get rid of chores and errands and miscellaneous phone calls so that you can relax and put your feet up for a time.

- Turn off all incoming access to you, including your cell phone, e-mail, and handheld device.
- Send out-of-office e-mails to your regular contacts.
- Stop the newspaper—and maybe even the mail—for a week and you will find extra time for yourself by not engaging in these routine but time-consuming activities.
- Invest in hotel-like amenities such as great sheets. They will be much cheaper than staying in the Four Seasons, and they'll have a long life in your household, too.
- Don't cook. Instead, have dinner delivered every night during your at-home vacation.
- Send out your laundry for the week.
- If a particular chore has really been bugging you, such as basement cleanup, hire someone to come and do it for you. You'll feel wonderful afterward.
- Relax outside by candlelight.
- Camp in your own backyard—with your kids.
- Have a three-day film festival at home. Establish a schedule for viewing films you want to watch and pick them up at the library or rent them from your local entertainment rental store.

■ Go on a vacation reading binge. You've set aside the time, and you can stretch out in the shade in the backyard or relax on the couch. Ignore the rest of the world this week.

■ Hire a massage therapist who makes house calls.

■ Have a yoga retreat in your living room. Buy a video or hire a yoga instructor for an in-home visit.

part

four

make time at the office

from the paper burden to

everything electronic

16

a work space
that works

So what does a functional work environment have to do with finding more time for yourself? Plenty! I can only estimate the work hours that are lost because people can't find what they need. The more time you spend on a paper hunt, the less time you have for yourself. Your work takes longer when you are disorganized.

One of my favorite stories is one I heard recently. An attorney worked at home two days per week, but she couldn't use her home office space anymore because it had become too cluttered with papers and files and case-related books. She'd taken to bringing her laptop to the dining table to work, but as you can imagine, that area was quickly becoming a mess as she brought in files and spread out her papers. The only real solution was a full home-office clean out, and the attorney eventually hired a professional to help out.

From observing my clients, I can tell you that people waste an average of thirty to sixty minutes per day "prospecting" for various papers. There's no doubt about it: a messy office wastes valuable time that could be used to get your work done so that you can leave in time to have a few extra moments of your own.

your office: solutions to eight common problems

"I panic when someone calls and needs information," says one client. "I'm always afraid I won't be able to find what I need for them when I need it."

When I visit offices, I see a never-ending stream of clutter. Because computers, cell phones, and handheld devices have increased the pace of our work lives, it seems there is less and less time to spend managing the papers and related materials that still arrive in every single office I've visited. (Most companies are still a long way from the goal of a paperless office.)

Businesspeople could add valuable time to their day if they would declutter their offices and set up a streamlined environment. This would entail eliminating unnecessary paper by reducing what was on hand to only the essentials.

Although many top executives pride themselves on maintaining neat desks, others are equally proud of their clutter. "I can find any paper I need here," most boast to me as I peer behind them at stacks of paper on the floors, on their credenzas, often on the couches, too. While this may be true, he or she is still using a lot of mental energy trying to remember where the papers for the Jones job are. This client could be using that energy for other things like finishing a report or preparing a speech or taking care of the small to-do items that mount up for anyone. (And if he or she is so certain the stacking system is so terrific, why was I called?) Consider how much easier it would be to simply file things under "Jones." (See chapter 17 for information on filing at the office.)

The well-thought-out office is comfortable and convenient and conducive to work. To find out how yours stacks up, perform an office checkup and modify any aspects of your space that are not working as well as possible.

1. *Are you distracted by people walking by your door?*

   Position your desk in the center of the office with the doorway to your side. That way you will be in a good position to welcome visitors, but you won't be constantly aware of the passing parade.

2. *Are you plagued by drop-in visitors?*

   You may need to replace a comfortable chair with a style that is less welcoming. Investigate wooden chairs or director's chairs—they are comfortable enough for an appointment, but not the kind of chair anyone would want to stay in for too long.

3. *Do you frequently run out of office supplies?*

If so, set up a system for your office. Put a clipboard in the closet or the cabinet where supplies are stored, and as soon as someone opens the last box of pens or paper or copier fluid, he or she should note on the list that a new supply should be ordered. An employee should be assigned to check the list weekly so that the office is aware when you are low, not out.

4. *When you are at your desk, are your files close by?*

Frequently used files should be in the file drawer of your desk or in a file cabinet within easy reach. Some people have a set of lateral file drawers right behind their desk that can double as a credenza. With a swivel of the desk chair, they have easy access to files they need. If file cabinets are far away, I find that people stack on their desks files that can be put away. It's a mess!

5. *Are you drowning in paper?*

You need to make time to weed out. You don't have to hold on to as much paperwork as you think you do. As a general rule, you can eliminate a great deal of what is on your desk and in your files.

If some of your mess is inherited from the person who held the job previously, do two things:

1. *Spend time getting to know the files.* People may call your office looking for things you didn't even know you had.
2. *Earmark items to go to dead storage.* If you are new in the job, you may not be knowledgeable enough about what to eliminate and what to keep, but getting it sent elsewhere in the building will make space in your office.

6. *Is your recycling bin nearby?*

It should be. The more paper you throw away as you go through the mail and old files, the less time you will have to spend managing it.

7. *Do you have shelving, and if so, what are you storing there?*

Shelves should be reserved for books and binders. Too often they become the home of stacks, which are an inefficient way of storing anything. Stacks of paper should be reviewed and placed in separate files where the papers can be stored in a dust-free filing cabinet and retrieved when needed. If you must save periodicals, try storing them between bookends in date order.

8. *How is your office lighting?*

If you are working under fluorescent bulbs all day, you might like to add a desk lamp to provide incandescent task lighting. Reading and file retrieval is faster because you don't have to strain to see.

your desk

Once you get your office in reasonable shape, the next challenge is your desk—and I've seen some real doozies. Take this quick quiz to see how your desk rates.

1. Do you frequently find your eyes drifting from your work to the other things that are out on your desk?

2. If you were to go through your to-do stack right now, would you find things that you should have dealt with several days or weeks ago?

3. Would it take you more than five minutes to look for a document you need immediately or that someone has requested from you?

4. Do you often come up blank when trying to figure out where a piece of paper should be filed?

5. Within the past month has the surface of your desk been clear and dust-free?

"I don't have time to straighten out my desk. I have too much to do, and it just ends up messy again," complain many of my clients. "Make time," I tell them. "You need a system, and you can clear out the paper clutter by devoting only fifteen minutes a day to the process. It is the single biggest time-saver you can give yourself."

Detailed next is a plan to get your desk organized quickly.

the fifteen-minute plan

Start with the tallest pile on your desk and begin working through it, evaluating each piece of paper and deciding what to do with it. Make one of the following three choices:

1. *Toss.* Unwanted mail, memos, and papers that should have been responded to but are now too old should be placed directly into the recycling bin.

2. *File.* Papers to retain should go directly into the proper file. This can be done easily if you followed the earlier advice to put your files within easy reach of your desk. (For more information, refer to chapter 17.)

3. *Respond.* If writing a simple response on the bottom of a letter or a memo will suffice, do so during your fifteen-minute decluttering session. If the response requires more time, place the letter in your collection of materials for tomorrow and add this task to your to-do list.

At the end of the fifteen minutes, stop working. (Your recycling bin should be overflowing, and your pile should be considerably smaller.) Take a look at your calendar and schedule in another fifteen-minute block of time tomorrow.

Schedule a pile review for as many days as necessary to get your desk down to the bare surface. Your goal is to achieve a clean desk with space for the following:

- Blotter
- Telephone
- Clock
- Calendar (if you use a paper system)
- Address book or roll file (if you use a paper system)
- Pencil holder containing pens, pencils, scissors, ruler, and letter opener
- Paper clip holder
- Stapler
- Tape dispenser

These items are generally used daily, so they should be kept within easy reach. Now that your desk is clean, you are ready to practice desk management. Create three file folders to help with managing incoming papers.

sanity saver

IN AND OUT EASILY

An in-box and an out-box are great ways to manage paper flow, but place your in-box on your credenza or on a shelf near the door rather than on your desk. (Or ask that coworkers leave papers and messages in an envelope-style pocket mounted right on your door.) If you have a direct view of the incoming work, it can distract you from the project you're working on. And no, a door system won't be within arm's reach, but you will maintain control of your paperwork by handling it when it is convenient for you.

1. *"To Copy" file.* Jumping up and down to make photocopies is a waste of time. If you need a copy of a document, place it in this folder. Delegate the copying if you can. If you can't, do your own copying at a time of day when the copy room is quietest so that you don't have to wait in line.

2. *"To Enter" file.* People always have information to enter into their computers. The best way is to save items throughout the day and do it all at the same time. As you come across financial statistics or names and addresses you want in your computer files, put the paper into the "To Enter" file. Then schedule time at the end of the day for making the entries.

3. *"Take Home" file.* Some people like to keep their briefcases close by and simply put papers directly into a "Take Home" file in the case. Others prefer placing papers in a file that gets transferred to the briefcase at the end of the day.

Files are an important key to office organization. Every time you start a new project, reach for a folder and label it for the new project. Even a project that must be completed in a day requires a folder. Afraid you will forget about it once it is filed? With your new time management system, you will write the project in your master notebook and break it down into the steps needed to complete it. (For more on your master notebook, see chapter 3; for more on filing see chapter 17.)

the neat desk rules

These rules will help preserve the order you worked so hard to achieve.

- *Maintain a clean desk surface.* The only items that should be on the surface of your desk are your desk accessories and the project you are working on. To achieve this goal, make it a priority to clear your desk every night before you stop working.

- *Process everything that comes into your office on the day it arrives.* Holding on to mail or memos is a guarantee of an office flooded with paper.

- *Don't accept what you don't need.* If papers that would be better handled by someone else arrive in your office, forward them immediately. You don't have to process what isn't there! One executive takes his own notes at meetings so that he doesn't have to bother with other people's notes or reports.

Set aside a regular time for doing paperwork. Come in early or stay late and have your telephone calls screened while you sort through the paperwork that, if permitted, is capable of swallowing up your desk.

When it is time to focus on your incoming paperwork, handle each piece of paper quickly and efficiently. Also, refile what you take out.

17

paperwork and filing

*M*ost people believe in saving papers; however, few seem to believe in filing them. In my work I have seen the unimaginable: beds, sinks, floors, corners, and closets stuffed with papers, and desks and tables stacked high with teetering piles of files.

What most people fail to understand is that the sole reason for saving a piece of paper is that you think you might have to look at it again. If you have papers piled in numerous stacks around your office—as many of my clients have—it's not going to be easy to retrieve the paper when you need it. This chapter will discuss how to store the paperwork you have to keep.

But first, let's give a tip of the hat to the Internet. It makes filing so much easier by cutting out certain paperwork from your life. If a salesperson has been to your office to see you and you tossed out the brochure he left you, you'll be able to find the information again on the Web. Or if you are looking for a great restaurant where you can take a client the next time you're in Seattle, you don't need to save articles and reviews—you can go online to find somewhere great. Or if you are considering investing in a new mutual fund, you don't need to save the booklet you received in the mail—when you have the money to invest, you can log on to the Web page to be certain that's the fund in which you'd like to invest.

In today's world, less really is more. Keep what you need to, file it intelligently, and you'll soon find that you have created more time for what you want to do because you will have fewer things that you *have* to do.

Here are three chaos-preventing maneuvers.

1. *Fully process each piece of paper that crosses your desk.* If you don't have time to answer a letter, annotate it with a description of what needs to be done and put it into a tickler file (discussed later). That way you won't have to reread or reevaluate the paper when you return to this item.

2. *Establish an* UNDER FIVE MINUTES *folder.* Place in it all the to-do items that aren't a priority and will take less than five minutes to complete. Leaving for lunch in a few minutes? Waiting for a meeting to start? Work from the UNDER FIVE MINUTES folder.

3. *File at the end of each day.* Slipping eight to ten items into a file will take only a few minutes if done daily. You may have to spend a boring hour on it if you wait until the end of the week. What's more, by filing regularly, you'll know where to find the paperwork you need, rather than wasting time by having to search frantically through a big pile on your desk.

The test of any good filing system is retrieval. Could you put your hands on a particular memo within three minutes? If not, then keep reading.

five easy rules for office filing

If you are going to get your paperwork under control, you have to set up a good filing system at work and stick with it, or like any system, it will collapse. Here are five simple ways to make your system work.

1. *Have ample space for the amount of paper you need to file.* Whether you are filing 15, 150, or 1,500 pieces of paper, you want to have enough space so that papers can be added to files easily, without stuffing. A good rule of thumb is to allow about four inches of empty space per drawer.

2. *Establish categories that work for you.* The headings you create for your files should establish an association in your mind that lets you retrieve what you have filed long after you have put it there. For example, if you have just purchased a new computer and want to file away the warranty and other computer-related information, COMPUTER is a more logical name than labeling the file according to the make of computer you purchased.

3. *File only what you need.* Many people save papers, articles, and documents "just in case." Before deciding to file something, ask yourself:

   Do I need to keep it for legal reasons?

   If I really needed to, could I find this information elsewhere? Remember that almost everything is available on the Internet.

4. *Be diligent.* File often and file regularly. By keeping up with your filing, you will find that the task will take only a few minutes.

5. *Maintain your files.* Create a system for cleaning out your files periodically, perhaps once a month, or each time you look in a particular file. Your files will remain more manageable and useful if you remove inactive or unneeded papers regularly.

choosing a system that works for you

Filing can be done by subject, by client name, or numerically (used in offices where privacy is paramount).

client name/color coding

For most people, a system that combines color coding with alphabetized file names (ANDERSON to ZIPP) or subject groups (all finance files together, all client files together, and so forth) works the best. These methods are easy to use and it's easy to identify the contents.

Color coding offers a strong visual association for retrieval. If green is the color you select for active sales clients, you will quickly see a green section within the drawer (hanging file, file folder, and file label can all coordinate). Blue can represent marketing efforts; yellow can be administrative files; red might represent urgent issues. Color coding makes it easy for others to keep up the filing system and helps ensure that items won't be misfiled.

When filing by client name:

Last name first

Followed by last names with just first initials—then last names with full first names

File with the exact name as a company uses it. For example, "North East" as a name versus "Northeast"

Ignore "the" in a company name when alphabetizing

subject files

Even if you primarily file by client name, you may still want some subject files for the following:

Correspondence

Records that are not specific to one individual or company

Newspaper clippings

Miscellaneous subjects such as "New Clients," "Paper Suppliers," or "Publicity Outlets"

If filing by subject, then selecting file names is the next important step. What you file will depend on how you select the subject headings.

sanity saver

HOW TO FIND A MISSING PAPER

- Recheck the file folder where the paper should be. Perhaps it's simply caught within the file.

- Now check the folders in front and in back of where this folder is filed. Perhaps the paper was simply misfiled.

- Is the information confusing, and therefore would someone have filed it under a different subject?

- Who else might have taken the file? Ask them if they have it.

When you select the titles under which you will file, be certain that the name is one that will remain meaningful to you. Ask yourself: "When and how will I want to retrieve this?"

numeric

If you need to use numeric filing, you and your staff will need to create—and have access to—an index book that can cross-index the file numbers by client name.

twelve additional time-saving filing tips

The initial effort you put into establishing a well-organized filing system is well worth being able to easily locate paperwork when you need it.

1. *When you receive a piece of paper to be filed, date it, note the source, and write the name of the file where it is to be placed.* You will avoid having to reread it to check its contents or what you intended to do with it. And if there is a time when the information will become obsolete, write "Destroy after _____" on the document.

2. *Papers that belong together should be stapled, not clipped.* Paper clips catch on other papers and lead to missing papers within a file. Special clip links can bolt hanging files together to prevent papers from slipping between the files.

3. *Don't pile.* If you are starting a new project, create a file for it the first day it arrives on your desk.

4. *Organize within the file.* The subject may break down into logical subject groupings: the file you keep on potential new hires might be divided up by the position for which you may hire, for example. If timing is important, an easy way to do this is by simply placing new papers at the front of the file. That way you have created a file that is sequential as to date.

5. *When your files become more than three quarters of an inch thick, it's time to break that file down into narrower categories.*

6. *Certain files may be more helpful if they are alphabetical.* When filing by name, put the last name first.

7. *If more than one person uses this filing system, create a master direc-tory listing all the subjects within.* Keep this list at the front of the first filing drawer for easy reference.

8. *If other people use a particular file, create a rules sheet.* The rules should cover how papers are to be filed and for how long items can be borrowed from the file.

9. *Have an "out" card system.* If you remove a file or a paper from a file for any period of time, leave a note as to the whereabouts of the item so that you will be reminded why something isn't there.

10. *File regularly.* People have different preferences. Some do it at the end of each day, which is most efficient for organizing your desk and your time and for being prepared for the next day's activities; others like to do it weekly. All people who have a useful filing sys-tem have one thing in common: they file regularly.

11. *Weed out frequently.* Whenever you have a file out, sort through it (this is a perfect activity to do when you are left on hold on the tele-phone) and toss what you don't need. On the inside of the folder, note the date on which you last sifted through it; that way you will know at a glance if you haven't been through the file in a long time.

12. *Within your filing system, create an area for inactive files.* Select one of the least accessible drawers for this designation. Every six months, cull through your current files and transfer those

---

sanity  saver

PICK UP SO YOU CAN KEEP UP

Every night remove extra papers from your desk so that the only thing on it when you return is the file pertaining to the task you are going to work on that next day. You'll be surprised at how inspiring (and calming) it is to come in to find a clean desk.

To accomplish this, create a folder for each task you are working on and store in it all paperwork and reference material related to the task.

you haven't used recently to the inactive status. This keeps the files easily accessible until you are positive they are indeed inactive and frees up space in your current drawers so that filing and retrieval is still performed easily. When you go through your files again in six months, those in the inactive area that are still untouched should be sorted again. Toss or recycle what you can and put the rest in a cardboard file box for storage outside your office.

conduct a filing check-up

If you are finding it difficult to locate many of the papers you have filed, use this system to conduct a checkup.

- *Are you up-to-date with your filing?* You would be surprised how many missing papers are found in to-file bins and drawers.

- *Are your labels hard to read or are the files worn out and catching on other things?* If so, it may be time to replace the labels and folders.

- *Are you using too many folders?* Many thin files are as complicated to look through as many single pieces of paper.

- *Are your files too stuffed?* If a folder gets too thick, the papers creep up and block the heading. If this is happening with any of your files, go through the file. Can you recycle or toss some of the papers, or should you create a new folder for the overflow?

- *Are your drawers overloaded?* When you access a file within a drawer, the drawer should not be so stuffed that it's hard to retrieve or return the file. If you don't have extra space in each drawer, you need to weed out.

tickler (or reminder) files— vital for the office

The tickler file system is a great time-saver that reminds you of what you need to know when you need to know it, without bogging you down ahead of time. (To save you time, I'll run through its office application here, although the system was introduced in chapter 1.)

The system described here is an actual set of file folders. After you note down that you are attending a conference next month, what should you do with the papers that outline the schedule? Put them in the appropriate tickler file, of course. While computers now permit us to enter date-related reminders of events, projects, and deadlines, it's still helpful to have a file system for the backup papers that go with these reminders.

Tickler files are the perfect way to manage papers that are temporarily important. The system provides a logical way to locate needed items as well as to remind yourself of things you must do or calls you must make on a specific date in the future. Here is how to create your office tickler system.

- Select thirteen file folders and labels. To color-code, select a specific color for this group of files. Label a folder for each month; label the thirteenth folder THIS WEEK.

- Clients in office settings often like a tickler file for each day, so in addition to the monthly set, take thirty-one additional folders and mark one with each date.

- These folders are where you will put papers that require action you don't intend to take care of today. Some examples include the following:

  Driving directions to a conference you are attending in three months belong in the folder for the appropriate month.

  A letter you have written that you will need to follow up on if you haven't heard back within a month should go in next month's file.

  Reminders to make an appointment for your annual physical, a mammogram, an eye exam, your six-month dental visits—each occurring at different times of the year.

18

e-mail, computers, and cell phones

When it comes to the new electronic gear we're all using, I sometimes wonder whether these items are time-savers or time-wasters. Of course, when my teenagers are able to call me on their cell phones with an update of when I should pick them up, or when I'm able to call a business client from the road to say I'm stuck in traffic, or when I can zap a quick e-mail to a newspaper reporter doing a story on getting organized or check an address on the Internet of a new restaurant I want to try, then cell phones and computers—and access to the Internet—are wonderful time-savers.

But when I can't figure out why my computer program has frozen and I spend forty-five minutes on the help line trying to get it unstuck, or my cell phone rings with a chatty friend just as I'm about to sit down for a few minutes of peace, then I begin to wonder if they are time-wasters.

Maybe the answer is both.

Whatever your viewpoint, these new inventions are definitely here to stay. From people chatting on the phone on planes that are being held on runways to parents thumping on their handheld e-mail devices during children's soccer games, we are a society that can't—and won't—turn back the clock on electronic inventions. A wife of one of my clients noted, "It's actually improved our marriage now that he can be plugged in at all times, and the handheld device for e-mail is far and away better for us than when he just had the cell phone." When I expressed surprise that she liked the office interference at all, she said, "Now that my husband knows that the office can literally get him information at any moment, he relaxes and enjoys the kids' activities. If his staff needs him, he'll step away and handle it. Otherwise he's there to have a good time."

So here's my advice on making certain that you save time—not waste it—while using these amazing devices.

e-mail management

We spend a lot of time on e-mail. According to a recent estimate, the average worker spends forty-nine minutes per day on e-mail; the estimate for management is closer to *four hours* a day; some of that time is from home or from wireless handheld devices.

Although e-mail saves us time and has made life much more convenient, it can also rob you of time that you could spend doing something else. For that reason, it's important that you find ways to make the time you spend on e-mail as efficient as possible. If you are using e-mail wisely, it is the perfect tool, and you won't become a slave to it.

Here are some basic tips to help you use e-mail more wisely at home and in the office.

- *Use discipline.* Deal with e-mail messages once. When a message arrives, read it and either respond to it, delete it, or file it away in a folder—but deal with it on the spot. If you let the messages linger, they create clutter or get lost.

- *Register for a good spamblocker program.* Junk e-mail wastes your time, so spend the money necessary for a program that blocks your computer from spam and viruses. The program will recognize about 75 percent of spam, but you will have the capability of identifying spammers that have gotten through and then the program will know to block them in the future.

■ *Organize your in-box.* You don't store canceled checks in your home mailbox, nor should you use your e-mail in-box for storage. Keep it cleaned out by sorting messages into folders.

■ *Automate.* Create a signature file—of your name, title, phone number, Web site, and e-mail address—to automatically appear at the bottom of your e-mail.

■ *Preview messages.* You don't need to open all your e-mail. Check the subject line and then the preview function so that you can scan and delete without actually opening the e-mail.

■ *Go wireless.* Wireless options include PDAs or one of the new cell phones that offer built-in e-mail access. Prices on both the devices and the services are dropping, and you can save time using a wireless device because you can check your e-mail anytime.

■ *Delete in bulk regularly.* Unless you are on a major company server, computers slow down when the hard drive gets overly stuffed with e-mail, photos, and Web attachments. By emptying your DELETED ITEMS and SENT ITEMS folders occasionally, you can keep your computer running a little more smoothly. Put any messages you want to save in a folder.

■ *Establish separate accounts for business and personal e-mail.* It's more efficient, and you will be able to focus better on both by doing so.

The When of E-mail Management

■ *Manage e-mail on your schedule, not on an as-it-arrives basis.* Check e-mail when you first arrive at the office, and then establish four or five specified times throughout the day to scroll through your in-box: perhaps at 11 A.M., right after lunch, mid-afternoon, and at the end of the day. Disable any of the alarms—those annoying pinging sounds—that ring whenever an e-mail arrives. These alarms are very distracting and will fracture your concentration.

■ *Delete spam and jokes immediately.* Spend prime morning time answering only the e-mails that are the most urgent.

■ *Respond to nonurgent e-mail when you are taking a mental break or are too tired to do priority work.*

The How of E-mail Management

- *Process your e-mail efficiently.* If it's about something important, let the person know the message was received, even with just a quick "got it!" reply.

- *Don't let e-mail pile up.* E-mail clutter is no better than paper clutter. Try to go through all the messages that come in every day, placing heavy emphasis on "delete," particularly for forwards and jokes.

- *If you can't get through all your messages some days, make an appointment to do it later.* Set a time on Friday afternoon or on the weekend when you can go through and clean out. Lots of newsletters now arrive by e-mail, and just like paper ones, you either need to make time to read them or delete them when outdated.

- *Create folders in your mail management program.* You can then slip important messages out of your in-box and over into work project folders or folders for various organizations you belong to.

- *Assign one folder as a TO ANSWER folder.* When you get a newsy e-mail from an old friend and would like to send a more lengthy answer, slip it over to your TO ANSWER folder. (You should check that folder about once a week.) And many experienced e-mailers would actually say that if you're extremely busy, it may be better to send your friend a three-line reply immediately. Sometimes waiting to have the time to write a more complete letter means that it becomes one of those tasks you just never get around to— and you risk hurting your friend's feelings in the process.

- *Create rules for some of your regular e-mail messages.* For example, most of us have some regular e-mail messages (daily or weekly) or some e-subscriptions that we enjoy or need to see. However, messages that arrive frequently slow us down in processing the more immediate incoming personal or business messages. You can set your mail program to handle some of this problem for you. First, create a separate folder for the e-mails you want to set aside—perhaps a SUBSCRIPTIONS folder, or perhaps a folder for a specific client's e-mail that you'd prefer to have set aside. Then go to the "rules" command. You'll be able to identify what e-mail messages should be directed into which folders, and from then on, the mail program will categorize those messages and you can deal with them when you are ready.

- *Get your e-mail in-box back to empty as frequently as possible.* Send what you can't process to the TO ANSWER folder so that you follow up later on.

When Sending E-mail

- *Be sure to fill in the subject line with wording that will appropriately move the message forward.* "Update" is meaningless, unless you provide more information on who or what you are updating.

- *If you are e-mailing someone who does not know you well, clearly identify yourself, perhaps in the subject line.* Don't assume your receiver will figure out who you are.

- *Use proper English in business e-mail messages.* Also include a greeting at the beginning of an e-mail and some type of closing at the end. Although Americans do tend to be casual about most things, a too-casual or overly friendly business e-mail may set the wrong tone. Follow proper etiquette until the other person has sent you a more casual response.

- *Be brief and get to the point.*

- *When responding to an e-mail, always restate what it is you are answering.* In a business e-mail, it is better to write complete sentences as you would use in a real business letter. With personal e-mail, cutting and pasting from the original e-mail is okay. Don't assume people will remember what they asked to which you are replying yes or no.

- *Minimize unnecessary e-mail traffic.* Between 10 and 30 percent of all e-mail messages are unnecessary, and sometimes, it's a matter of politeness gone awry. If you don't need to hear back from someone, introduce colleagues to the EOM or "end of message" system. Let them know they don't have to send a reply.

- *Avoid copying messages to others.* Send your messages to people on a need-to-know basis.

■ *Avoid requesting receipt of sent e-mail.* Some e-mail programs have the option that you can receive a receipt that someone has opened your e-mail. Unless you really need to know an e-mail was received, don't request a reply or a receipt. You may need to disable that feature—it's annoying to the recipient.

■ *Avoid using* PRIORITY *and* URGENT *tags.* Use them only when absolutely necessary. These tags make it seem as if you don't trust the recipient to understand that your message is important. (And people who tag their e-mails in this way usually aren't tagging anything that is actually very important.)

■ *Be careful of expressing sarcasm, humor, or irritation in an e-mail.* Messages that are both written and read in haste can often be misinterpreted.

■ *Create a template for messages you send frequently.* This saves time as you don't have to create from scratch e-mails you send on a regular basis.

■ *If you're mailing to a list, use the BCC function.* This hides the names of your recipients to provide them with privacy. Put your own e-mail address in the "to" area to hide the recipients' contact information from one another.

■ *At work, don't clog up your company's server with e-mails that contain attachments or jokes.*

■ *Don't put anything you might regret in an e-mail.* Remember, too, how easily e-mail messages can be forwarded—accidentally as well as on purpose. Ask anyone and they'll tell you a horror story about an e-mail they wrote that was forwarded—or sent —to the wrong person. That definitely can cause sleepless nights!

■ *Be careful of keywords.* Companies pay someone to create software programs that scan messages for keywords that might mention something illegal or that might indicate that someone is spilling company secrets. About 45 percent of companies monitor employees' electronic communications, according to the American Management Association, and that figure is expected to rise. Programs vary widely from those that can protect financial companies to those that are guarding pharmaceutical secrets to those created to prevent leaks to the press by companies that interface with movie stars. E-mail messages sent at work can't be withdrawn. Once they hit the company server, they become scannable company property that can be used for anything from a court case to a reason to fire you or a colleague. Offensive or insulting e-mails can be grounds for a workplace lawsuit.

■ *Humor and anger are two e-mail troublemakers.* The e-mail you dash off and think is quite funny may be misinterpreted by someone reading it quickly. If in doubt, don't send. The same philosophy applies to e-mail messages written in anger. Reread the message carefully. Is there anything about the e-mail message you are sending that could cause trouble down the line? If so, then you probably shouldn't send it

■ *The delete button is not as good as you think it is.* Files are released from your vision but not from your hard drive, and almost any electronic data can be retrieved if necessary. Bear in mind that you don't want something to come back to haunt you.

■ *Never assume your e-mail is private.* You have little control over what someone else may do with any e-mails you send.

E-mail Management when Traveling

■ *Never let e-mail pile up if you can help it.* If you have a handheld device, then you can read and send messages when stuck on a plane or waiting for your rental car or at the hotel check-in desk. If you don't have wireless e-mail capability, you can still check e-mail while you're away. Sign up for one of the free Web-based e-mail accounts that checks all your POP e-mail accounts automatically. You'll sign on using your POP server name, user name, and password.

■ *Consider a universal in-box.* These permit you to access both voice and e-mail messages over the Web or by phone. Typically, voice mails arrive as audio files that you can listen to while e-mails are read to you over the phone by a virtual assistant. Fees can vary from $5 to $20 per month, and some services charge by the call. Check www.webley.com, www.i-link.net, www.messageasap.com, and www.linxcom.com

organizing your computer for maximum efficiency

Here are some easy-to-implement tips that will save you time when working at your computer—and you don't have to be a computer geek to set them up!

- Newer is better, so if you're beginning to think your computer needs updating, it's probably time for a new system. A new, faster computer will help you work more efficiently.

- Most people today want Internet access at home as well as at the office. Go for the fastest system in your area. The expense is well worth the investment in time saved.

- Find a good computer geek (a professional—you don't want to let a high school student learn at your expense) whose number you can keep on file. Whether you need him or her to help you with setting up a new machine or you just need someone to come by for some technical cleanup, a pro can finish in under an hour a task that a layperson might spend a full weekend on.

- It isn't *whether* your computer will crash, the question is *when*. It can't be said too often: *back up*. There are excellent software programs that can be set to back up your data regularly to a disk or a tape or—if you're on a network—to another computer. Trying to recreate what was on your computer is truly a nightmare—ask almost anyone. We've all had it happen.

- Also make certain you've taken care of virus protection and update it according to the software company's recommendations. Whatever you spend on the virus protection software is worth it; hiring someone to come in to undo viral damage is costly and very frustrating.

As for managing the computer itself, these tips will keep your machine, your documents and files, and you operating effectively and efficiently.

- When was the last time you cleaned out your Internet "favorites" category? This system was designed to save time, but if you have fifty favorites—many of which you no longer use—then you aren't saving time. Go through and evaluate which marked sites are still your favorites. Delete the others from your list.

■ Just as a hard copy in-box must be kept under control, so, too, must the e-mail in-box. If you don't monitor this in-box, it becomes like a never-ending to-do list, sure to give you a stomachache because it's guaranteed to grow exponentially. Once a week, go through all the in-box messages. If you really need to save some of them, create folders (under your computer's in-box heading) and move the e-mail message into the appropriate category. You can create folders for each client or for various projects, or use subject headings that are meaningful to you. If you are too busy to deal with a particular e-mail message (or several of them) print them out and read them while waiting at your next appointment.

■ When it comes to document storage within your computer files, think "folders, folders, folders." Name them carefully, and if one folder becomes overloaded, remember that you can create subfolders within a category.

■ To cut down on computer clutter—and to protect the information— copy the previous years' financial information onto a CD and store it in a safe place. Better yet, create two CDs. Store one at home and one at work so that you'll always have a backup copy and then delete the files from your computer.

■ If you use the Internet frequently and would like to track what Web sites you've visited and what you found there, explore some of the new software programs like MS One Note. You can copy text and graphics from Web sites and the program automatically stores a hot link if you want to return to the site.

■ Fax without a fax when you need copies of signed documents. Save the expense of a dedicated fax machine by signing up for eFax.com or MessageASAP.com or a similar service. These sites provide you with a fax number that can receive and forward faxes to your e-mail account for you. The document arrives as an attachment, and you can print it out from your computer.

■ One of the best search inventions offered by several search services is the ability to locate documents within your desktop computer files. Remember how frustrating it used to be to "know you've already written the body of the 'new employee' press release" but not know where you'd filed it on the computer? Today you can search a few keywords and desktop search engines will bring up every document and every e-mail as well as every Internet site with that string of words. You know you created that list of great European restaurants that you wanted for your next business trip—now search for just one restaurant, and you'll soon be able to put your hands on the document. This new tool can save you hours.

- If you juggle between multiple computers (home and office, or office and laptop), then you'll save time with a new form of software that permits total synchronization of selected files via the Internet. Working on a draft of a report at the office? When you open the file on your laptop on the plane, the exact same version will be there. Dataport methods or e-mailing documents to yourself have solved this problem in the past, but you had to plan ahead to have the right files with you. Two programs for consumers are BeInSync for Windows XP or Windows 2000. FolderShare can operate on both Windows and Apple Macintosh.

cell phone management for optimum use

Cell phones are a great tool for saving time and making your life easier you can conveniently keep in touch with your family, the office, and your customers. Effective phone use will enhance your business, but poor habits reflect badly on you.

If you've ever puzzled over what your phone is actually capable of, then you will fully appreciate the first piece of advice about cell phone use in the following list.

- *Read the manual!* In this day and age, no one reads the instruction booklet, and yet, cell phone makers have made them reasonably easy to read. Afterward, you'll actually know what your phone can do. You may also be surprised to learn that your phone has many more features than you thought, and probably never would have imagined having on a phone.

- *Check out cell phone companies on the Internet.* The Web sites will provide you with updated information on companies' respective cell phone models. This is an excellent and easy-to-use resource and a great way to supplement information.

- *Know how to reach customer service.* Note the number of your cell phone service provider, which usually offers a toll-free number for those in need of tech support or who have customer service inquiries.

calls control

Here are some suggestions for managing your cell phone so your callers don't manage you.

- *Don't let your cell phone rule your life.* Don't be compulsive and answer every call, anywhere, anytime. Turn off the phone during important family time and during nonbusiness hours when you don't want to take calls. Use voice mail, and return calls promptly at an appropriate time.

- *Focus on the people you're with, not those who are calling.* When you're with customers or colleagues, give them your undivided attention. Avoid answering incoming calls. Don't compromise a great sales presentation or other business interaction by being a slave to your cell phone. Remember, the person you are with is your most important customer at that moment. If you allow an interruption, it sends the wrong message. Your voice mail will capture any important calls, and you can follow up later.

- *Stay on task and in meetings.* Never allow a call to interrupt a meeting. If the meeting is important enough to have on your schedule, it's important that you focus on the meeting, not on your next phone call.

- *Control your costs—and be considerate.* Even the best calling plans cost money and time. Keep your calls focused. Don't make calls just because you have free minutes or free time. If there's little to discuss, don't make the call. What might be free time for you could undermine the productivity of the person receiving the call.

- *Do one thing at a time.* Don't engage in complex conversations while driving, or while doing anything else. Both your clients and other drivers on the road deserve attention. If you are on the road a lot, invest in a hands-free headset. Statistics show that any kind of distraction hurts your driving response, but realistically, people are going to talk and drive—just do it hands-free, and remain aware that your first priority must be your driving.

- *Be considerate of others and maintain your privacy.* When you talk on your cell phone in a public place, everyone within earshot is a potential eavesdropper. Worse yet, some cell phone users believe they need to shout to be heard. Talking loudly in restaurants, in movie theaters, on buses, and in other public places is rude and disruptive—and there are some business and personal conversations that should not be overheard by others. If you must take a call in a public place, excuse yourself and move to a private location.

- *Back up the numbers on your phone.* Most people have dozens of numbers stored on their cell phones. Cell phones can and do get lost, so use a computer program to make a backup copy of the phone numbers. Several companies offer programs that let you save the numbers into a file on your personal computer.

19

office systems
and shortcuts

*T*his far into the book, you have been introduced to all the principles of managing your time at home and at the office. If you're like most of my clients, what you need is to brush up now and then.

"I do pretty well most of the time," says one of the executives I've helped. "But late in the day, it's a lost cause. E-mails are flying, my desk is getting buried, and my brain is almost nonfunctioning."

This report is typical. We all get "fried brain" toward the end of the day—too many things happening, too much multitasking. This client and I actually worked out a system that let her recharge. About 4:30 P.M., she goes outside and walks around the block. (And no, she doesn't take her cell phone or her handheld device with her!) When she comes back in, she's calmer, her brain is clearer, and she can then spend another hour and a half or so finishing up her work.

Like this client, you need to figure your own way to give yourself a mini-break so you can get things back under control. My intention in this chapter is to provide you with shortcuts, speed systems, and other ways to help you get things done more efficiently. The chapter even includes another idea or two for a mini-vacation—take them when you can!

A few subjects—such as conducting a time-efficient meeting—are unique to the office and deserve special attention. Most of the other information shared here is based on what you have already learned in previous chapters, but I'll remind you of these ideas by applying them to business.

office triage

There's not an office I've entered that doesn't operate in crisis mode much of the time. To overcome this, act as if you were in an emergency room—triage your priorities.

Deal with the most important items first—this generally means focusing on your biggest or best client, or selecting a task in order of what brings the most money in the soonest. Depending on the situation, you might ask what support task needs to be accomplished to help you bring in more money? All other work should be a lower priority. Delegate what you can and fit in the low-level work at low-productivity times (the end of the day, generally).

meetings

If you are scheduled to attend a meeting:

- Note in your planner what time you need to leave your office to arrive on time for the meeting.
- Find out if you are required to stay for the full time if it is a long meeting covering several subjects.
- Take with you something to do in case the meeting starts late.

If you are organizing a meeting:

- Hold meetings only when absolutely necessary, and keep them brief.
- Schedule breakfast meetings. They tend to be shorter and allow people to take action on meeting goals and deadlines on the same day.
- Prepare a written agenda so that people come prepared.
- Delegate note taking so you can focus on running the meeting.

- Energize office meetings by keeping people on track. Don't let people wander with their comments.

- Have index cards on hand at the meeting so that everyone can write down their notes or assignments.

delegate whenever you can

Delegation allows you to function at your best and to give your full attention to more important tasks.

- Develop your staff and train them so that they'll be able to do the jobs you need them to do.

- Supervise for a time before turning someone new loose on a new task.

- Don't allow upward delegation.

- Create a delegation record to keep track of what you've handed out. Set deadlines for the work that you delegate.

getting through business reports

Business reports are important but can be tedious to create. Here are ways to make short work of them.

- Give each report a quick glance. Decide right away whether you should read one immediately, or whether it can wait. If it is a priority, write it in your master notebook. If not, put it in your reading file.

- Skim the material so you will know the direction the piece is taking.

- Read the first and last paragraph of the full text you want to read. This often gives you a summary of what the article is about.

reminders, reminders, reminders

The following reminders are all things you may know, but I find that my clients often forget to heed these helpful time management practices. Use a highlighter while reading this section to mark the advice you tend to forget.

quick  start

WHAT YOU CAN DO . . .

In five minutes, you can

- Read your mail.

- Set up your calendar.

- Create a guest list for a business reception.

In ten minutes, you can

- Write a letter or a memo.

- Scan a newsletter.

- Give yourself a brain break.

In thirty minutes, you can

- Skim a report and mark parts that need to be read again more carefully.

- Read journals and newspapers that you haven't had time to get to.

- Start one step of a complex problem.

- Go to the office early to knock off some small tasks before the day gets under way.

- Take care of your top priorities while you are still fresh.

- Preserve time for priority work by blocking visitors and phone calls for short periods of time.

- Ask that your staff separate your mail into "priority" and "routine."

- Schedule times when you can go through your mail and e-mail.

- Use a highlighter when reading letters to those parts requiring action.

- Throw out as much as possible.

- Don't write when a phone call will suffice.

- With phone calls, get to the point quickly. Encourage others to do so, too, by saying, "How can I help you?"

- Make minor decisions quickly.

- Eliminate unprofitable activities. That committee you serve on may no longer fill the need you or your company once had. Give the chairperson notice of your resignation so he or she can replace you.

- Is there a crisis happening? Figure out a long-term solution to the problem.

- Don't shuffle papers. Try to touch each piece of paper only once.

- Purchase and learn to use time-saving equipment such as the various features of your cell phone, your laptop, your handheld, and different computer software (for example, contact manager–type programs).

- Always confirm appointments; don't assume the other person will remember.

- If someone calls for an appointment, try to settle the issue on the phone before setting up a meeting.

- Don't store magazines. Tear out or photocopy relevant articles and discard.

- Don't read passively. Search for ideas. Use a highlighter to mark important sections. Make notes in the margin.

- Use colored flags to mark important sections as you read.

- Put into binders newsletters or bulletins you might want to look at again.

- Don't share office supplies, or they may not be there when you need them.

- Always carry a small pad for recording notes.

- Carry sticky-backed notes so that you can jot down reminders to yourself wherever you go.

- Carry a portable three-hole punch in your briefcase so you can organize as you go. Office-supply stores sell thin ones that can be snapped into a three-ring binder, adding very little bulk.

- Keep a pocket tape recorder with you for recording quick thoughts.

- When you take a business card from someone, note on the back how you are supposed to follow up or what you need to remember about the person.

- Include your assistant's name and number on your business card so that people will ask for him or her instead of you when they call.

- Subscribe to one of the executive book summaries programs to save time but stay informed.

- Download audio magazines and books onto an MP3 player and listen to them during your commute or while exercising. Audible.com uploads a great deal of new content each week, ranging from *Forbes* to the *Harvard Business Review*.

- Does someone want your help with something? Your involvement should be based on your goals—not your availability.

- Be decisive.

- Don't use your desk as a giant in-box.

- De-junk. Eliminate desk clutter. The picture frames, the what-nots, the in-box, the papers, and all the office tools (stapler, letter opener, pencil holder, and so on). I visit clients who store so much stuff on their desks that it's a wonder that they can get anything done. (I guess they realize that or they wouldn't hire me!) Lots of items people don't even notice anymore. I'll say to a client, "When was that picture taken of your child playing soccer?" and he will answer: "Soccer? What picture?" These items need to be shifted to an off-desk location, and even some of the tools such as the stapler or letter opener may fit neatly in a drawer.

- Eliminate excess paper whenever you can.

time booster

WHEN SOMEONE SAYS, "HAVE YOU GOT A MINUTE?"

After you hear that person's question, ask yourself:

- How much time will it take?

- Could someone else handle this?

- What am I supposed to be doing that might be more important?

- Start a file for any new project.

- Don't save paperwork you aren't willing to spend time filing.

- Use your calendar (electronic or otherwise) to overcome the "if I put it away, I'll forget about it" worries. Choose a date when you want to be reminded of a task or a report, write the reminder on the calendar, and file the paper away.

- Learn to say no.

overcoming feelings of stress

It is perfectly natural to have down times during the workday. The workplace can be overwhelming and stressful at times. If you sometimes find yourself fading out and unable to function well, consider the power nap. Leonardo da Vinci, Winston Churchill, Albert Einstein, and Thomas Edison were all nappers—and studies show that napping actually helps productivity. A NASA Fatigue Countermeasure Program study found that airline pilots who napped, on average, for as little as twenty-six minutes experienced a 34 percent improvement in performance and a 54 percent improvement in alertness. Unfortunately, the National Sleep Foundation survey found that only 16 percent of adults say their companies allow naps. That said, there is no reason why you can't catch a few winks in your car at lunchtime on a particularly fatiguing day.

Stress on the job can lead to decreased productivity, increased frustration, and irritability. To de-stress:

Use humor when you can.

Stay focused on the positive.

Take your shoes off.

Take deep breaths.

Even if you can't nap, make sure to take breaks during work time. Getting up and walking away from the desk for even five minutes can freshen your thinking and help your body cope with stress.

Once you are home, give yourself a complete break.

Turn off your cell phone while you are decompressing.

Do yard work.

Enjoy watching television or reading.

Take a yoga class.

Be sure to remain involved in nonwork-related pursuits. You need to have hobbies, sports you love, and friends to be with.

Here are some time-saving tips to help combat feeling overwhelmed.

- Replace face-to-face meetings with conference calls or online sessions.

- Divide professional reading among colleagues. Then let each person point out anything particularly important.

- Move deadlines up. Depending on the timeline, consider telling yourself (or others) that certain things are due one week before the actual due date.

- When appropriate, leave detailed phone messages to reduce the need for phone tag. The next phone call will be more productive if the other person can retrieve what you've asked for before calling back.

- Before beginning a new project, take the long view of the undertaking so you understand the ultimate goal. Then plan and structure the steps that will get you there.

- Set a one-month limit on your reading material. I've seen clients who "clip and save," but that pile, too, can become overwhelming.

when you have to work late

It is inevitable that you may occasionally have to work late. Depending on the industry you're in, your position within the company, and your own work habits, staying at the office past quitting time may be a frequent occurrence. Regardless of whether working late happens once in a while or nearly every day, here are some things you should be aware of.

- Know your company's overtime policy. Sometimes companies will specify that a certain amount of notice must be given—although pointing this out on the afternoon when he or she has asked you to work late may make your boss angry.

time ( ) booster

RELIEVE STRESS AND GAIN ENERGY THROUGH EXERCISE

Make exercise a priority no matter how busy you are. Exercise is an underrated time management technique that makes you more energetic, alert, and creative.

- Ask your boss if you can take the work home and finish it there.

- Check with your caregiver regarding his or her flexibility to stay late on short notice. If your caregiver has other commitments or has to get home to his or her family, arrange backup help.

- Pick up your child and bring him or her back to the office with you for an hour to do homework while you finish up.

- Coordinate with neighbors or friends who might help you out— perhaps you can return the favor in a different way.

- Consider the fact that sometimes you'll just have to say no.

- Have a dinner in the freezer for whoever will cover for you at home, and have something you can heat up quickly once you get home.

if you work at home

Working at home has its pros and cons. To make the best of this situation requires planning, structure, and supportive family members. Here are some ground rules to keep you productive.

- Set specific office hours and stick to them except in an emergency. In addition to providing a structured work environment for you, establishing work hours also provides a set system for family members so that they know when you're available and when you aren't.

- Some people set up a definite routine for beginning work. I have some clients who take a walk after breakfast or establish a routine trip to buy the newspaper, and when they come back they act as if they are arriving at work rather than home. If you experiment, you'll find a ritual that works for you.

- Establish routine buffer time at the conclusion of your work. Turn on the news, go to the gym, do something with your kids. Creating a habitual way of ending the workday will help you draw the line between home and work.

- When you do take time off from business for something personal or to go to a school event, don't feel guilty. Establish a set time for making up the hours you lost. Tell family members that you'll be working Saturday morning to catch up.

- When you leave the office at the end of the day, close the door. There's nothing worse than walking by your office and being reminded of all the work you have to do.

- Draw boundaries that remain firm. Having a separate business telephone line adds to the separation of work and family. If you're not working, don't answer the business phone.

- Avoid reading for pleasure in your office or playing games on the work computer. Likewise, don't bring work into family parts of the home. Make certain that the office is for work, and your home is for leisure.

- Reclaim your nights. Many people go back to work after dinner, and eventually they feel burned out. They're no longer keeping up with their hobbies, and they've lost the knack of relaxing with the family. It's important that you maintain a personal and family life as well as keeping up with your work.

- Take vacations. Everyone needs a change of scenery now and then, and the home-based worker in particular can use one.

part

five

make time
you and your family

20

family systems
and shortcuts

Kids are wonderful, but they take up a lot of time! Though a child will absorb every single moment you can give to him or her, remember that you are of little value to yourself or your family if your energy is depleted by burnout.

When I sometimes have to meet with clients in the early evening, I am always reminded of why that time of day for families is known as the "witching hour." As a mother of three children who are a little older but still at home, I still experience nights in our household that are quite stressful—too much homework, too much laundry, dinner in progress, the phone ringing. It's enough to drive me mad. But when I visit families with young ones I am reminded of whining and tantrums and neediness and little hands not capable of helping out—and a bone-tired emotional and physical fatigue that cannot be explained to anyone who doesn't have children.

Getting organized and instituting specific systems for the morning, for the evening, for getting out of the house on time, and so forth *does* make a difference for busy families. What's more, it's absolutely vital that you set an example for your children of being organized and managing your time. In this day and age, it is imperative that children learn these things.

With the number of demands—and the number of electronic distractions or temptations—already pulling at them, all hope for an orderly life will be lost if they don't learn to set priorities and manage accordingly.

Although all the principles in this book are applicable to family life, this chapter will provide you with some specific ways to streamline the family's needs. In the process, you will accomplish two things:

1. You will uncover a little extra time when you may be able to grab a break for yourself.

2. You will be more likely to spend your time with your children at the park instead of picking up puzzle pieces or performing other time-consuming, unrewarding chores.

encourage independence

As your children become more independent, you will find that you need to invest less time in maintenance chores, so you will have more time for the fun part of parenting. To help guide them:

■ Help children help themselves. Purchase small pitchers for milk and juice, and keep them on a lower shelf of the refrigerator. Always have healthy snacks readily available.

■ Fold and store outfits together. This is a real time-saver when searching for matched sets. As children get older, show them how to do it for themselves.

■ Teach young ones the valuable lifelong habit of keeping related items together—from stationery to toys to puzzles to athletic gear. Children need to learn early on how to maintain order.

■ Do you want to instill organizational skills in your children? There is no better way than setting good examples of everything from weeding out to neatening up—not to mention the art of managing time. Children learn by what they see.

calming morning mayhem

Mornings can be hectic—the kids need to get ready to go to school and you have to get ready for work and your day. But there are relatively simple ways to make mornings less chaotic.

- Wake up enough in advance to have a few minutes of your own—to exercise, skim the newspaper, or just catch up where you feel you're behind.

- Do as much as you can the night before. Help your children get their clothing chosen and laid out, set the breakfast table, unload the dishwasher, sign permission notes, get homework back into backpacks.

- Create a morning routine so the kids know what to expect. They will function much better with one.

- Encourage short hairstyles to simplify the getting-ready process.

- Eliminate morning power struggles by limiting choices: blue shirt versus green or corn flakes versus hot cereal.

- Lay clothing out ahead of time. Give younger children simple choices between two outfits.

keeping children's rooms tidy

One mother called me because her son's room didn't "work" anymore.

"He used to be relatively tidy," she said of her thirteen-year-old. "I don't know what happened."

She then led me to his room, where it was very clear that the kid didn't have a chance. He was beginning to stretch out like a string bean, and of course, he required longer pants and bigger sweaters, and he favored shirts that were oversized. Yet his mom thought his clothing could still be put away in the wooden dresser they had used in his room since birth, and the closet was still configured for the hanging of toddler-size things.

Parents often fail to realize that children's rooms might need makeovers. Organize children's storage space so that it will hold clothing and possessions that are appropriate to their ages. Families also need to rethink the floor plan of children's rooms. What worked for a seven-year-old won't be suitable for him once he's fourteen or fifteen.

And even if you've realized this, you still have to help your child do a spring cleaning, or a good sorting, every twelve months or so. Over time, even the best organizational systems fall into disarray, so schedule a yearly room checkup. Clothing and toys and books should be sorted through annually, too. With your child, decide whether to rearrange furniture or make other changes. (Before the winter holidays might be a good time for this sorting in preparation for "out with the old, in with the new.")

- Before undertaking any of the sorting, think through the changes you'd like to make. If your son wants an aquarium, where will it go? He'll need to understand that trade-offs are usually necessary in creating room for something new.

- For young children, allow for play space as you plan out the room.

- Put erasable message boards in children's rooms. These can be handy for children ranging in age from toddler to teen. Write on them reminders of items that need to be taken to school, homework that needs to be done, and chores that are awaiting attention.

- When sorting, children age six and over can probably work alongside you, but they will probably do best if assigned specific tasks. Younger children will be delighted by some of the treasures you unearth, but to do the tossing you may need to send them off with their other parent for lunch.

time ⏲ booster

HELP YOUR KIDS FIND TIME

Do you feel that your kids are wasting time on the computer or watching TV? Before you create a new rule for them, remember that everyone deserves some relaxation time, and television and computers games are big favorites.

If you feel your children spend too much time this way, set up a system to monitor their screen time. For example, introduce the concept of "appointment television." At the beginning of the week, let your children plan what they would like to watch so they get to see a few favorite shows, but they aren't glued to the set indefinitely.

Computers and computer games should be ruled by the clock. Whether you decide to allow thirty minutes or an hour and a half per night for electronics, set your family rules and then stick by them.

Desk Area

- Good lighting, a desk, a comfortable chair, and bookshelves are essential to providing a good study area.

- Save important papers in files.

- Track lighting eliminates needing to put a lamp on a desk or a dresser.

Bed

- Simplify bedmaking. Use fitted sheets and a comforter and limit the number of throw pillows or stuffed animals that are part of the bed décor.

- Hang mirrors at children's height on the back of the closet door.

Closet

- Hang clothing on an adjustable pole at children's height so they can reach items easily and put their own things away. Adjust the poles as the kids grow.

- For children sharing a closet, divide the pole in half by painting each portion a different color.

- Store out-of-season clothing, linens, sleeping bags, or overnight bags in the upper part of the closet.

---

sanity  saver

SAVE YOURSELF!

If your children are driving you crazy (and they are old enough not to need constant supervision for safety reasons), send yourself to your room for ten minutes, announcing that you will be in a better mood after you have a few minutes to calm down. And guess what? You will. A few minutes of reading, meditation, or closing your eyes will make you feel better. By the time you return, the children will likely have calmed down, too.

■ Sort clothing and shoes frequently. Kids grow quickly! Be tough about what you save for a sibling. Coats, boots, and good-quality clothing are okay to save, but T-shirts tend to discolor and become gray over time. Pass them on to someone sooner rather than later. What you save for a younger sibling should be labeled according to the age or the year when you think it will be handy.

Toy and Book Storage

■ You'll spend less time cleaning up after your children if you have a family system for picking up after each different activity. Exceptions can be negotiated for items like a block city. How many days will you permit it to remain before the floor under it needs to be vacuumed?

■ Group and separate toys, and dedicate bins to various types of playthings.

■ Create storage in attractive colored boxes and bins. Sorting is an essential developmental skill. Post a picture of the toys that go in each bin so even nonreaders can help put things away.

■ Assign numbers to puzzles and write each puzzle's number on the back of all the pieces so you that you can quickly put them away together.

■ Keep a big plastic basket in the garage for outdoor balls and toys. Use a pegboard so that kids can hang up skates, baseball gloves, and other outdoor toys.

■ Devote a specific part of a bookshelf to library books. Write the due date on your calendar, and once that day comes around, you'll know exactly where the books are.

homework made simple(r)

Homework can often be a challenge, even for the smartest kid. Here are some ways to keep you and your kids on top of this important aspect of academic life.

■ Find out the homework policy at the beginning of the year, and create a homework box or a desk area with necessary supplies. Talk to your child about when he or she will do homework, and then be around (in person or by phone) to offer encouragement when necessary.

- Stockpile school supplies including poster board, covers for special reports, and colored markers, so that you can avoid last-minute trips to the store for items your child needs for a school assignment.

- Keep all homework supplies in one place. Older children capable of working on their own may have desks in their rooms where these materials can be kept.

- Younger children are better off working near you. Consider buying an inexpensive set of drawers on wheels for storing the supplies. Inexpensive plastic drawer systems are available at hardware and houseware-type stores. If your child does homework in the kitchen while you're fixing dinner, the drawers can be rolled to the table for a work session and then put away when it's time for the family to sit down for a meal.

- Teach long-range planning. When your child starts getting long-term assignments, teach her how to break down a project into parts. Then use a calendar to show her how to look forward and estimate how much of the project must be done by a certain date. Note on the calendar when each part of the project must be completed to finish the assignment on time.

- Trade off on who helps with schoolwork. It can be a good parenting time, and each parent brings something special to the experience.

---

time ⊙ booster

ENGAGE DAD

Get Dad to help out. Even in this enlightened age, working women are still largely responsible for looking after their homes and families. In 1998, women age twenty-five to forty-four employed full-time with a spouse and at least one child under age nineteen at home spent 4.9 hours per day on unpaid work activities. This is an hour and a half more than their male counterparts, who averaged only 3.3 hours per day on these activities.

- "Dad, can we go to the library?" says Susie, who now mentions she has a report on dinosaurs due the next day. This type of question used to be guaranteed to cause an adult's blood pressure to rise. But now, no problem. Most school districts or public library systems have created Web-page links accessible from home that offer a large quantity of school-approved information. School Web sites sometimes break the links down according to age so that the first grader researching dinosaurs isn't looking at the same material that is appropriate for high school students.

> sanity  saver
>
> ### SCHOOL NOTICES
>
> To make certain you return school notices, post on a bulletin board an open-ended envelope that you can slip the notices into until it's time to take them back.

birthday fun

Why any adult in his or her right mind would sign on to have thirty to forty kids come to a birthday party is beyond me. Chaos can be the order of the day unless you employ good sense.

- Make the birthday party small. Invite one guest for each year of your child's life, plus one.

- Keep it short. One to two hours is plenty of time.

- Enlist helpers. Whether these are high school kids you hire to help out or your sister and mother-in-law who volunteer their services, be sure you and your spouse have extra hands for the party.

- Keep it simple. The younger the child, the simpler the activities should be.

- Order party favors online. Unless you live or work near a great store where you know you'll find trinkets at the right price, buy online. You'll be able to watch prices better, and there is sometimes a bulk discount if you're ordering a dozen or more items.

child care

Using others to help take care of the children is absolutely vital to anyone who has children and would like a little time and space for themselves. For most of us, the grandparents no longer live around the corner, so the next best option is hiring someone to help out. Whether you need full-time help because you work, or want to hire a regular babysitter so that you can pursue some of your other interests, here's a brief overview of the process.

- Before starting the hiring process, you must:

    Define the job and think through the hours and responsibilities.

    Decide on the most important qualities for your household right now—good with babies; able to manage a toddler; willing to do housework and pet care, and so on.

    Set the salary, decide benefits and vacation. (Talk to experienced friends and coworkers about what they've done. Full-time day or live-in workers should receive one to two weeks' paid vacation after one year of service. Live-out employees typically receive six paid holidays per year; live-in, eight. As for sick days, five or six paid sick days may be in order.)

- Call the Internal Revenue Service (or stop by your local office) and ask about any general information they have about in-home employees. You'll need information on obtaining an employer identification number and instructions on filing a Form W-2 for taxes and Form 942 for Social Security payments. If you pay $1,000 or more to a home-worker during a calendar quarter, you are required to pay federal unemployment tax (FUTA), so also ask for information about Form 940.

- Also contact your insurance agent about whether you need to carry workers' compensation insurance. Nearly half of all states require it for domestic help now. If your agent doesn't know, he or she should call the state labor department to investigate. (Premiums on household employees are generally not costly—less than $150 in many states.)

- Find your candidates by letting your friends and family know you are looking to hire a child care worker. Sometimes their

sanity  saver

KEEP THEM HAPPY WHEN YOU
NEED A FEW MINUTES

Every parent knows certain things set off a child. Whether your daughter just hates it when you leave or whether your son becomes whiny when he knows you have to make phone calls, there are ways to make these moments more peaceful.

- Create activity bags that get taken out only for special purposes. A travel bag, a telephone bag (for when you're on the phone), and even a babysitter bag (special favorite items for when you're going out) will help amuse your child at a time when he or she may be distressed that you are on the phone or leaving.

- Create an art kit out of a big rubber bin. Buy one that's only about four inches deep so that supplies don't get buried. Then when the kids have nothing to do, you can get it out for them.

recommendations can lead you to a good prospect. You can also try agencies, read (or place) newspaper ads, and post the job on community bulletin boards.

- Save time by prescreening on the telephone. Prepare and photocopy a form that should be left by each telephone noting information such as language skills, enthusiasm for the job, where he or she last worked (and reasons for leaving), whether the person drives, and anything else that seems important to you. If the person seems like a good candidate, set up a time for him or her to come for an interview. (Be sure you have his or her phone number, in case you have to cancel or change the time.) Give specific directions to your home.

- At the interview, spend a few minutes chatting to put the person at ease. Next, go over some of the material you've discussed on the phone: responsibilities, hours, benefits, and what the starting salary is. Once the candidate seems comfortable, you'll want to find out:

Previous work experience.

Why he or she is seeking another job now.

Ages of previous children under his or her care.

Any specific expectations on his or her part—for example, needs to leave early on Wednesdays for night class.

Allergies, health problems? Does he or she smoke?

If you have a pet, will that bother him or her?

If the candidate has children, what provisions has he or she made for their care? What will he or she do if they are sick?

If you'll need to leave written instructions, verify that he or she can read by having a children's book available and asking him or her to read to your child for a few minutes before leaving.

- Check work permits and alien registration cards, if applicable.
- To get a better sense of the candidate, discuss potential household occurrences and how he or she might handle them. Choose one or two questions to ask (no need to overwhelm the candidate) such as: What would you do if my child refused to take his nap? What would you do if my two-year-old threw food at you? What would you do if she cries when I leave in the morning? What if my son ran away from you at the playground? What would you do if you smelled smoke in the house? What would you do if my child fell and the cut was bleeding quite a bit?
- Tell the candidate anything about the household you feel he or she should prepare for: "I sometimes have to work late, and I don't always know in advance. Would it bother you to work overtime on short notice?" or: "Having a neat home is very meaningful to me, so daily pickup is an important part of the job."
- Offer him or her the opportunity to ask questions.
- Observe the candidate's attitude when he or she meets your children. Even if they spend only five or ten minutes together, you'll get a sense of what type of person he or she is.
- Make a full set of notes on your discussion. You'll never be able to remember all the details after interviewing several applicants. Also

BE PREPARED

- Have a ready-to-go-at-all-times diaper bag. Pack diapers, wipes, bottles, a sippy cup, a plastic bag for dirty diapers, a changing pad, a hand puppet, a rattle or other small toy. Repack each time you get home.

- Keep a bucket of toys in the back of the car for long car trips or if you're stuck in traffic and the kids are with you.

- Take one of their favorite books with you if you may have waiting time at your destination.

- For the under-seven set, a hand puppet is a sure pleaser. These toys pack almost flat and are sure to amuse if you get caught with an unhappy child or too much time on your hands.

note your emotional response to the person. Did he or she seem wrong for the job, despite having all the right answers? Did you just love him or her?

- Check references! Find out about the length of time he or she was employed in previous positions, why he or she left, and what his or her attitude toward the job was.

- If you hire through an agency, most agencies do criminal background checks on the people they send out. You may want to ask about this.

- Your own inner voice should be the last one you listen to when deciding whom to hire to take care of your children. The nanny I hired when my oldest daughter was born stayed with us for five years. She was the first person I interviewed and the moment we met, I knew everything would work out. It did. All these years later, we still keep in touch.

summer vacations

As children finish the spring Little League season and participate in innumerable end-of-school events and recitals, most families look forward to enjoying those lazy, hazy, crazy days of summer—or so they imagine. Suddenly school is out, and all that free time is tough to manage.

With advance planning, you can not only rest assured that you'll still have time for things you personally want to do but you'll also find it perfectly possible to create quality family time. What we tend to forget is that most of us thrive on routine, and the beginning of summer brings a new routine. Here's how to adjust your family's schedule so that you can best enjoy summer for the healthy change of pace it should be.

planning ahead

Winter is the best time to start thinking about summer. Schedule a family meeting to include everyone in a discussion about what they want to get out of the summer. Here are some items you should consider in January or February.

■ If you're planning to take a family vacation, read through guidebooks and travel brochures to pick the spot. Book your hotel room or put down a deposit on a house rental as soon as possible so that you won't have to compromise on your preferences. (If it's too early for a deposit on a rental, at least you'll have decided on one or two and be first on the list of people to whom the house is offered.) If you'll be flying, you should also investigate air fares. Often, you can get less expensive rates by booking early.

■ Are your children going to summer camp? Some cities have camp fairs you can attend to get an idea of the programs that are available. If not, other parents or the school faculty may have suggestions. There are also reputable camp referral services; check the telephone directory Yellow Pages under "camps" for the name of one in your area. Most camps give tours at specific times during the winter, or if the camp is too far away to visit, they'll usually send videotapes or a representative may visit you to help you and your child make an informed decision.

- If your children are going to participate in area classes or programs, find out about programs during the winter and ask when registration is held. Some programs fill quickly, so you'll want to know how and when to sign up.

- If you are divorced and your children will be visiting the other parent, or if stepchildren will be coming to stay with you, talk to the other family as early as possible so that your plans can be set accordingly.

sanity saver

OUTSOURCE!

There are things you are no good at or hate doing, so outsource certain tasks. Hire someone else to teach your kid to ride a bike. Pros often promise they can teach it in a day! When it comes time to teach kids drive, hire someone then, too.

- After blocking off the "we're away" or "she's away" days on the family calendar, take a look at the days that are unscheduled. Do you need to plan for child care? Will unscheduled time hang too heavy on everyone's hands? (Unscheduled time in June when other families are still around is generally easier to manage than unscheduled time in August when many people tend to be away.) Teaming up with another family to share responsibility for keeping the children amused in late summer might be fun and advantageous for all.

when summer arrives

Once summer arrives, put your early planning into action.

- Develop a family tradition such as a trip to an amusement park or a picnic in the mountains for the first day or first weekend after school is out. Having a specific family event to look forward to can help children cope with the loss of their daily routine with school friends.

- Establish a new, looser daily routine, and do it as quickly as possible. (Remember that it will take at least a week to settle into a new routine.) One family found that a late-day outing—to the pool if they hadn't been that day, or an after-dinner walk in the park—was a new routine they all liked. Since homework and dance classes no longer filled the afternoon and evening hours, it was a pleasant way of breaking up the end of the day.

- Have school-age children set at least one purposeful goal for themselves each summer. It might be learning to dive or building a model airplane, but the focus on learning something new teaches self-discipline and gives them something to look back on with pride.

- Encourage reading. Check with the local library for programs and reading games that will be taking place during June, July, and August. Most children enjoy participating in library events, and they are a great way to keep books a part of kids lives during the summer.

- Consider altering a school-age child's chores for the summer. One mother expected her children (a boy and a girl) to take on one specific household task for the summer to see what different aspects of running a home were like. Starting when they were preteens, she taught them a new chore and expected them to be responsible for it weekly throughout the summer. One year it was laundry; another year it was vacuuming and dusting. In retrospect, the daughter's favorite was meal preparation. "We each took one day per week and were responsible for the family meals for a full day. I think I made them eat chocolate cream pie for dessert every week," said the daughter, laughing. "I think my parents were really glad when that summer was over." The maximum time spent on the chore each week was only about two hours, but the all-encompassing style of the responsibility (all the laundry or all the meals for a day) made for a valuable learning experience.

- For summer weekends, always have two sets of plans: indoor and outdoor, so that your activities are not totally weather-dependent.

summer fun as a family

Summers are the perfect time for creating those "remember when" family memories. Planning for a pleasant summer can help bring about the right atmosphere for those times that you'll never forget.

- Set up a dinner co-op with other families. Each family chooses one night to cook, then other families come by to pick up that evening's meal.

- Plan day trips.

- Catch up on putting your photos into albums.

- Visit with neighbors in the evening.

- Get up early on Saturday to get chores done, and then head out for a day of fun.

- Take off your watch. Not checking the time helps you slow down.

- Do volunteer activities as a family. From local walks to fund-raisers to cleaning up a park, spend time together helping others.

- Don't let the summer become overscheduled the way the school year often is. Let children have some time to hang out and find their own fun.

- Stop cable television service during the summer. See what it's like to live with diminished television options—or go cold turkey and tell the kids, "No television for the summer."

- Make the most of the time you have. Even something as simple as fixing dinner together can be extra fun if you devote the time to it.

saving memories

When your children first bring home their artwork, hang it on the refrigerator or establish a bulletin board where you can post items for a temporary time. Then before you remove the art, have your child-artist pose by his or her favorite pieces while you take a picture. This will give you a permanent record of their accomplishments.

Store special school projects and graded assignments that your children are proud of in a magazine file box or an art portfolio sold at toy stores. Twice a year (more often if your pile is growing), sort through and toss work sheets but save unique art or stories that will be fun to look at later on. Transfer those you want to save to a storage folder labeled with your child's name, age, and grade.

family memorabilia

Every family has special, treasured objects that they like to display and keep. However, it's important to develop a system for collecting, storing, and eventually weeding out memorabilia.

- Use the summer as an opportunity to weed through and toss some of the memorabilia that has been accumulated over the year.

- Display favorite times and store memorabilia that is not on show, sorted by person and labeled, in archival containers.

- Ideally, organize family photos as they come in. If you don't have time to put them in albums, date and label the photo envelope so that you'll at least have a general idea of what the contents are.

- For digital photos, don't rely entirely on the cyberspace storage systems offered by some photo companies. You should download your favorite pictures to your own computer (and back up your computer regularly). Families have been distraught when companies folded—or the family neglected to pay the annual subscription fee—and their online family photo albums were wiped out.

index